Tippecanoe and Tyler, too!

THE STORY OF WILLIAM HENRY HARRISON

TIPPECANOE AND TYLER, TOO!

by STANLEY YOUNG

Illustrated by WARREN CHAPPELL

RANDOM HOUSE · NEW YORK

First Printing

Published in New York by Random House, Inc.,
and simultaneously in Toronto, Canada, by
Random House of Canada, Limited.

Library of Congress Catalog Card Number: 56-5456

Manufactured in the United States of America

For

Great Chiefs Koo Koose Toby, Snowball Searle, High in the Sky Gary, Geoduck Mike, Roger Cropped Top, III, and the Little Moose Byles—along with Squaw Girls Ox-Alice Cathy, Katy Long-Braids, and other wild Indians I have known.

Contents

Introduction

In the small town of Battle Ground, Indiana, just north of the city of Lafayette, there is a towering white granite monument. It stretches ninety-two feet into the prairie sky and is surrounded by sixteen wooded acres and a high iron fence. Erected by the state and nation, the monument marks the historic site of the remarkable Battle of Tippecanoe.

Tippecanoe is the name of a river in Indiana. It is an Indian word, originally spelled Quittepeconnac or Kithtippecanunk, and it means buffalo-fish, a type of fish that once abounded in the wild river's waters.

Not as many Americans know about the Battle of Tippecanoe as know about Lexington and Concord, or Valley Forge, or Gettysburg, or the Alamo. Nevertheless, the gallant struggle that took place on the Tippecanoe River, November 7, 1811, between pioneer Americans and warring Indians, was of major importance in American history. Without this battle more than 200,000 square miles of our country might have been lost forever.

This vast wilderness region, west of the Allegheny Mountains and north of the Ohio River, was known then as the Indiana Territory. Out of it later were carved the great states of Indiana, Illinois, Michigan, Wisconsin, and part of Minnesota.

But in 1811 there were only about 25,000 settlers in the entire Indiana Territory.

The adventurous few who pushed West were in constant peril of Indian massacres. The Indians, often incited and aided by British and French trappers, contested, foot by foot, the coming of the Americans. In the Indiana Territory there was constant strife: border scalpings, raids, cabin burnings, and wholesale massacres of pioneers. For years William Henry Harrison, Governor of the Indiana Territory, had patiently tried to keep peace with the Indians of his region. Finally he was forced to take up arms against them. In the battle that resulted along the Tippecanoe River, the power of the daring Shawnee chief, Tecumseh, and of the last great Indian confederacy east of the Mississippi, was broken—forever.

After the battle Harrison's name became forever associated with the crucial encounter. Thousands of Americans of that day began to call him "Old Tip, the hero of Tippecanoe." When, later, William Henry Harrison ran for President on the Whig ticket with John Tyler, the campaign slogan was "Tippecanoe and Tyler, Too!" The whole country knew what the slogan meant.

Yet few living Americans today know the whole story of the gallant soldier and administrator whose life-size statue looks out over the Tippecanoe River and the famous battleground where, so many years ago, he saved so much of America.

For the full story, we must go back nearly two hundred years.

Tippecanoe and Tyler, too!

THE STORY OF WILLIAM HENRY HARRISON

1 · *The Young Seeker*

William Henry Harrison, the hero of Tippecanoe, was born on February 9, 1773, at "Berkeley," Virginia, a large and pleasant plantation on the James River in the county of Charles City. Here, for his first twelve years, he roamed the deep woods and explored the broad river with only his older brother, Carter, his sister, Sarah, and the slaves' children for companions.

As there were no schools near the plantation, William Henry took all his lessons from a private tutor, Mr.

Ethan Randolph. He was a stern but thorough man who lived with the family. Mr. Randolph instructed all the Harrison children five days a week in Latin, Greek, arithmetic, literature, and history. At the insistence of William Henry's father, who was a strong believer in education, the tutor sometimes threw in a smattering of geography and astronomy on Saturdays, and two hours of Bible reading on Sundays. William Henry, at this time, was said to be an attentive but not an exceptional student.

His parents were often disappointed in him. They were well-to-do and of distinguished heritage, so naturally they expected their son to excel in whatever he did and to show signs of being able to carry on the family's good name.

"All during my youth my father admonished me about my studies," William Henry wrote later, in a reminiscent moment to a friend. "Father also spoke long and frequently of our family background. I think I was twelve when he called me in and said formally, 'Billy, I should like to tell you about the Harrisons. The first Harrison came here early—1632—and settled in Jamestown when the colony was little more than a settlement, with Indians all about and the comforts of civilization not to be had. This first Harrison in America was the descendant of a famous British general, and was most active in the affairs of the new colony. . . .' "

Doubtless Benjamin Harrison also told his son about the other Harrisons in colonial America and the Bassetts on his mother's side. Members of both families had, from the beginning, taken important parts in the political and military life of the struggling colonies. None, so far as is known, ever returned to England.

Benjamin Harrison, William Henry's own father, had been one of the most distinguished of the Harrison clan. As early as 1764, eleven years before the Revolutionary War, he had joined a committee that sent a strong protest to the British Crown about the unfair taxes imposed on the American colonies by the Stamp Act. He could have been hanged for this act of rebellion, as he very well knew. But Benjamin Harrison was a fearless man and a staunch champion of freedom.

No doubt William Henry, as a growing boy, was not fully aware of his father's many public acts of patriotism. But in later years he was fond of telling stories about his bold parent. He particularly liked the story of how his father first got John Hancock of Massachusetts to accept the office of Speaker in the Continental Congress. When John Hancock modestly refused the honor, Benjamin Harrison picked up the reluctant Mr. Hancock in his arms and carried him bodily to the Speaker's chair amid roars of laughter and approval from the other delegates.

With a father so active and prominent in politics, and with the new country's leaders—men like General Washington, Robert Morris, and Benjamin Franklin—so frequently at "Berkeley" as guests, it was expected that William Henry would develop an early interest in political life. But this was not the case.

Though he is said to have listened attentively to the lively talk at his father's table, what William Henry liked best was the study of medicine. All through his boyhood he "played doctor" to the entire plantation. He was never happier than when he was bandaging the wounds, real or imaginary, of his brothers and sisters and the family servants.

Even the plantation animals came under his young care. It is reported that at the age of twelve he set the broken leg of a pet colt so satisfactorily that the horse doctor, when he finally arrived, had nothing more to do except to pat William Henry on the head.

To encourage his interest in medicine—the single interest he had shown at this time—William Henry's parents sent him at an early age to Hampden-Sidney College, in nearby Prince Edward County. But when he was sixteen he left Hampden-Sidney because his parents were displeased with the religious instruction of the school. He continued his studies, for a brief time, at an academy in Southampton. Then, after a summer in Richmond, where he stayed with his brother Benjamin and worked as an apprentice to a Dr. Andrew Leiper, he was taken to Philadelphia. Here he was entered in the school of medicine under the instruction of Dr. Benjamin Rush.

Philadelphia, when William Henry entered it in 1790, was a bustling city and the new country's capital. The public squares resounded with gossip and rumor and the latest news of stirring events throughout the young nation. Stagecoaches clattered in and out of the city laden with mailbags and important visitors. Government couriers, with secret dispatches in their saddle-pouches, galloped by on sweating horses. Soldiers were everywhere in the streets, marching by in high boots, the sabers of the officers flashing in the sun.

Young William Henry, straight from his quiet life on a plantation, must have been excited by all this activity. Going back and forth through the cobbled streets to his medical classes he passed daily the regimental drilling grounds and army headquarters. Certainly he could not have missed the weekly military parades, or the huge bulletins posted in the public squares calling for emergency volunteers to the army.

President Washington himself had issued the bulletins. They had been brought out immediately after the President heard of the growing peril of the Indian border wars along the Ohio River. All Philadelphia was talking about the border massacres and scalpings, and anxious about relatives who had migrated to the West.

Whether William Henry, at this time, was stirred by a sense of patriotism, or only by a sudden restless wish for adventure, is not known. His father had died suddenly on April 25th, 1791, and the boy had been placed under the able guardianship of Robert Morris, the Philadelphia financier. In October, 1791, when he was eighteen and his second year at medical school had barely begun, William Henry announced to his mother and guardian that he wished to volunteer for the army.

Both William Henry's mother and his guardian quickly opposed his decision to volunteer. "It's foolhardy, Billy," his mother wrote from "Berkeley." "Your medical course comes first. Besides," she added, doubtless hoping to frighten him, "you might get killed."

"Precisely," Robert Morris agreed, when William Henry showed him his mother's letter. "This Indian warfare is most hazardous, Billy. Frontier life is scarcely the life for a young gentleman."

But William Henry was not to be put off so easily. He informed his elders that he had already written to General Knox, the Secretary of War, and had also made an appointment to see President Washington to apply for a commission. His mother was dismayed, even as she secretly felt proud of her son's resourcefulness.

"Billy is somewhat delicate, even spindly," Robert Morris assured Mrs. Harrison privately. "Possibly he will not be found acceptable to the army."

William Henry apparently did not share this doubt about his health and strength, though he might well have. A full-length portrait of him from this period suggests, at first glance, that he was physically unsuited for the rugged life of a frontier soldier. The portrait shows a long, thin, sensitive face, beardless cheeks, ears that stick out a little too much behind his thick sideburns, and a lanky, somewhat awkwardly spare figure—all arms, legs, and bone. A closer look, however, reveals a determined cleft chin, a stubborn set of the head, and a fearless pair of deep-set eyes. The final impression is of a strong spirit and an equally strong will shining out of a frail body.

"I reckon it's not the way you look, sir, that makes you a soldier," William Henry is reported to have said to his guardian. "I reckon it's more what you do."

Robert Morris's reply is not recorded. But evidently he protested no longer, and advised Mrs. Harrison to give in to her son's determined wish, for the next thing we know young William Henry was on his way to his memorable interview with President Washington.

2 · *Appointment with President Washington*

William Henry must have approached his interview with much nervous excitement and with considerable pride in the fact that he was able to get to see the busy President. All his friends at medical school surely knew he was going to be presented to the grand old General in person—"the Father of our Country," as everyone around Philadelphia called President Washington.

William Henry had waited weeks for the appointment.

Of what actually happened at this famous meeting we can only gain hints from William Henry's later writings. "I rose early that October morning. I dressed carefully, in my very best apparel."

Again, from the portrait, it is easy to imagine what must have been his "very best apparel." Doubtless he wore his tight velvet jacket, with the lace cuffs that stretched down over his long arms, and possibly his knee-length pantaloons, and his polished square boots with the silver buckles. Certainly he must have taken his heavy greatcoat and his wide-brimmed, three-cornered hat to protect himself against the chill autumn air.

But what were his thoughts as he sped down the stairs from his room and across the mud-splashed streets to the office of the first President of the United States? Did he have any fear or misgivings?

"How I wished, at that moment, my father were alive to go with me!" William Henry admitted years later in a letter to a friend. "I was fearful that President Washington would consider me a nuisance, as only another pestiferous son of a distinguished father who wanted a favor. Looking backward on that momentous day I wonder whence I summoned the boldness to present myself. Ah, the courage of youth is a glorious thing! It springs, no doubt—at least in great measure—from youth's happy inability to foresee difficulties. I am less bold now by half."

William Henry goes on to say how, on that morning, he stood stiff-spined and rigid, "to keep my knees from knocking," as the fifty-nine-year-old Washington came forward and cordially shook his hand and called him "Mr. Harrison."

President Washington recalled his visits to William Henry's home in "Berkeley" and spoke of the time he had dangled William Henry on his knee. Then he politely mentioned William Henry's father. "I am exceeding sorry to learn of your father's untimely death," President Washington said gravely. "He was a great patriot and a great Virginian." The President fixed his calm, steady eyes on William Henry. "No, you don't much favor your father as to physical resemblance, but I trust you have his character."

"Yes, sir," William Henry stammered, doubtless feeling his tongue too thick and heavy for his mouth.

What else was actually said can, in part, be imagined from William Henry's further statement that "the President talked with me at considerable length about my plans for the future, about his own youth in Virginia, the rigors of military life, the pressing problems of the new Northwest Territory—all before touching on the matter for which I had come. I thought him, at this time, much older and graver than I had remembered. Yet his dignity, force, and general bearing were most impressive. I resolved in my heart to model my own life, as best I could, after his."

There is no doubt, then, that President Washington bolstered William Henry's interest in military life. The President probably stepped to the wall map above his desk and pointed out to William Henry the Northwest Territory—that vast wilderness that stretched from the Great Lakes to the Ohio River. This was the land that the British, Indians, and French were trying to keep for themselves. Yet this territory was, according to the Treaty of Paris in 1783, rightfully American. President Washington was determined to defend and preserve this land for settlers and for new states. That is why he had asked for a volunteer army immediately.

He had a memorable interview with President Washington.

"The Secretary of War informs me there is a commission open in the artillery," the President said to William Henry, as he took up a letter from his desk and examined it. "If you will kindly see the Secretary, I shall be pleased to sign the commission on your behalf." He stood up and held out his hand. "I trust you will be of service to your country and worthy of your good name. Good day, Mr. Harrison. My kind remembrances to your mother."

The President courteously conducted William Henry to the door. "When I was your age," he added, with his hand resting on the polished oak doorknob, "I was a surveyor in western Virginia. It was a new land, then. Nothing but Cherokees, Creeks, an occasional Iroquois Indian, and a few trappers. And plenty of bear and deer. That's where I learned about the wilderness and Indians. I thought it a pretty rough life. But the experience, I might say, came in pretty handy later—against the Redcoats." He smiled again, his slow warming smile, as if he were remembering things far away. "Good fortune to you, Mr. Harrison. I trust you will rise to a high station in your chosen profession. You go with my blessings."

"Thank you, sir," William Henry managed to say, then found himself outside.

As he stepped into the corridor he felt his knees trembling again. He hadn't said any of the things he had meant to say. He hadn't told the President that he knew all about General Josiah Harmar's terrible defeat by the Indians, and how he needed recruits.

In the whole interview about all he had said was "Yes, sir" four times. Had he even thanked the President for his commission? Yes, he remembered. He had at least done that!

He was so excited now that he took the wrong turn in the long curved hallway. It was several minutes before he found the office of the Secretary of War. There was a uniformed guard outside who saluted him smartly as he went in. The salute almost made him feel that he was already a soldier.

The Secretary of War drew up the proper military papers as William Henry waited impatiently outside with the guard. Immediately the orders were dispatched by messenger to President Washington's office. In half an hour the orders came back, signed and sealed, and were delivered over to William Henry.

When he got outside, he looked at the papers. Yes, it was all true! The papers plainly read:

William Henry Harrison, Esquire, is hereby commissioned to the rank of Ensign in the Army of the United States.

By order of,

GEO. WASHINGTON,
President of the United States of America.

Clutching the papers under his greatcoat, William Henry hurried toward his quarters, splashing his way through puddles of rain and mud that he no longer noticed.

When he got to his room he read the papers again, more calmly this time. They stated that he was to report for duty the next morning at the army's headquarters in Philadelphia.

He yelped for joy, and flung himself headlong onto his cot. How lucky he was! A commission in the Army of the United States! Now he was one of 5,400 picked men. He wondered suddenly if Dr. Rush would think him a fool for deserting his study of medicine to become a soldier.

And what would his brothers, Benjy and Carter, who had fought in the Revolution, think? And Sarah, his twenty-one-year-old sister? Dear Sarah, who had played "captain" to his "colonel" all during the war-games of childhood. He would have to take up his quill pen and write them the thrilling news at once.

He hauled out his wicker traveling box from under his cot and started to pack, jamming everything in helter-skelter. No need of his broadcloth coat now. Nor his spanking-new pantaloons. Nor his shiny shoes with the silver buckles. He would have a uniform soon, and great knee-boots, and maybe a saber.

That night he went to bed early. But he was a long time falling asleep. Already it seemed to him as if he were taking part in the new life that lay just ahead. Already he saw himself in battle against the Indians on the great western frontier.

3 · *Journey to Two Forts*

Ensign Harrison spent the next four weeks in the Philadelphia garrison learning to become a soldier. He had been told that his training period would be three months, so he was unprepared when his commanding officer suddenly called him in and said, "Ensign Harrison, you are to march eighty recruits to Fort Pitt. From there, you will proceed to Fort Washingon on the Ohio."

"Yes, sir!" William Henry answered. He gave the captain a quick salute that barely hid the grin forming at the corners of his mouth.

Fort Pitt! That was a two-hundred-fifty-mile march westward, across Pennsylvania! And Fort Washington? He dug out his map. There it was, far down the Ohio River at a log settlement called Cincinnati. He grinned again. Yes, this was fine. This was action, and what he had been waiting for. No more dull drilling and marching, drilling and marching, up and down, back and forth, in the same square field. Now when the recruits marched they would be going somewhere!

The next morning Ensign Harrison and his men and ten mule-drawn supply wagons swung out of Philadelphia, headed for the Lancaster road. The soldiers were all in fine spirits. And why not? The fife was tootling, the drum was rolling, the muleteers were cracking their whips, and the girls waved gaily as the soldiers swept by.

Ensign Harrison and his men marched briskly four abreast. "Left, right. Left, right. Left-left, I-had-a-good-job-when-I-left. . . . Left-my-wife-and-fourteen-children, hayfoot, strawfoot, Johnny-got-a-haircut, Left—Left . . ." They stepped off twenty miles the first day, and no one felt the worse for it.

But by the fifth day the orderly marching broke down. The roads had narrowed to rutty trails, and the men, strung out in single file, walked in weary, uneven strides alongside the jouncing supply wagons. Often the heavy wagons mired down in the thick mud. At such times William Henry had to order his men to heave-to with all their strength to get the mules on their feet and the supplies rolling again. They were carrying precious kegs of gunpowder as well as food, so it was important to be extra careful.

By now, of course, their new uniforms were splattered with slush and dirt, and scraggly beards had begun to darken their faces. As the sturdy stone houses of the Dutch farmers became fewer and fewer, and the green line of the forest grew deeper, they all began to realize that home was far away, perhaps behind them forever.

"When d'ye think mebbe we'll see Injuns, sir?" one of the men up front asked Ensign Harrison.

William Henry looked at the smudged, clay-stained face before him, then glanced down at his own grimy uniform and his calloused, work-red hands. "Not between here and Fort Pitt, I reckon," he said. Then he grinned. "But looking around, I'd say most of *us* are beginning to look like savages!"

Harrison and his men walked on, often making no more than twelve miles a day. They had to ford swollen autumn streams and skirt fallen trees. Sometimes they stopped to forage for game when they grew tired of their monotonous camp diet of salt pork, tea, and hominy with molasses. Promptly each day at sunset they made camp. They slept in their uniforms, their black felt hats over their faces to keep out the smoke from the fire, and, at sun-up, staggered to their feet again to start another day.

William Henry had plenty of time to think as he tramped along. He wondered a good deal now about the career he had chosen, and where it would lead him. Would he do anything important? Anything that would be remembered? Or would he get scalped, maybe, or else just turn into a tired old soldier in some lonely wilderness outpost?

He remembered suddenly what his father had told

By the fifth day the orderly marching broke down.

him about the other Harrisons—men who had made names for themselves. Now that he was beginning his own career, these dim ancestors began to assume a reality in his mind and to arouse his curiosity.

When he halted his men for supper he could hardly wait for an opportunity to bring out the Bible his mother had given him. On the fly-leaf, in his mother's elegant handwriting, was a record of the family's history.

As he glanced down the page, he saw at once that his father had been the fifth Harrison in America. He had almost forgotten that. He turned to the beginning. Yes, here was listed the first Harrison of Jamestown about whom his father had talked so much. What was so important about him? He read the brief notations quickly. "Served on the Council of Virginia. Aided the Governor in ruling the new colony."

Next came the son of that first Harrison. This son had also been on the Council and a soldier besides. William Henry smiled to himself, pleased. Another soldier among his ancestors. He read on. The second Harrison in America had also had a lot to do with starting the first college in Virginia—a college called William and

Mary. William Henry was astounded. Why, that was the college where his own father had studied!

He moved on to the record of the third Harrison. This ancestor had become attorney-general, treasurer for Virginia, and served in the Colony's lawmaking body, the House of Burgesses. But he had done something even more important for the family. One day he had rowed up the James River and bought from Governor Berkeley the property where the Harrisons now lived.

The fourth Harrison, William Henry knew, was his grandfather. Another soldier! But when he wasn't fighting, he had been a farmer. He had built up the family plantation, and finally served in the House of Burgesses, too.

It was most impressive, William Henry had to admit, being related to all these great men who had served their country so well.

"Take my own father," he said to himself, as he stirred the wood fire before him. "Everyone agrees that he was a great man, even President Washington."

Not only had his father sat in the Continental Congress during the dark days of the American Revolution, but he also had been a signer of the Declaration of Independence. Along with Mr. Thomas Jefferson and Mr. Benjamin Franklin, he had been one of fifty-six men chosen to sign the great document that had founded the country!

There was a framed copy of the Declaration above the fireplace in his father's study. William Henry had read it, and he remembered now some of the solemn words above the fifty-six quill-scrawled signatures: "And for the support of this Declaration, with a firm reliance on the protection of Divine Providence, we mutually pledge to each other our Lives, our Fortunes, and our sacred Honor."

His father had gone on to become a speaker in the legislature, and governor of the grand old state of Virginia. Governor Benjamin Harrison! That was certainly something to be proud of!

And then William Henry turned the page to his mother's family. He guessed they must be distinguished, too. At home he had heard much talk of the proud Bassetts. As soldiers and public servants the Bassetts had worked for the new country ever since 1660.

Yes, it was most impressive, William Henry repeated

to himself. But it was a little frightening, too. He couldn't help asking himself whether or not he would ever measure up to this fine family name and heritage. He wanted to, but he was worried by the thought of failure. All he had now was a sword, a tattered uniform, a scraggly fifteen-day set of whiskers that itched, and badly aching feet! Not very encouraging. Well, there was nothing he could do right now but march on, and hope the future would somehow take care of itself.

By the time he sighted the Stars and Stripes fluttering above Fort Pitt, William Henry and his company had been traveling twenty-one days. They were dirty and footsore, but actually they all looked worse than they felt. The aches and pains they had groaned about during the first days of their march had disappeared. They had, little by little, become toughened and sobered by their new life in the open. Their faces were tanned now, their muscles hard, and their stomachs flat—a little flatter, in fact, than they wanted them to be.

"Aye, but they're all real soldiers now!" Ensign Harrison thought with pride, as he looked over his ragged band of recruits.

With the Fort in sight the men whooped, waved

their hats, and quickened their steps. Even the weary mules seemed to sense that the journey was almost over, for they snorted out a series of resounding "hee-haws" that echoed down the valley. The soldiers laughed and, out of good spirits, began to imitate the mules, "hee-hawing" at one another to see who could raise the loudest echo.

William Henry, now that his first military assignment was ending, suddenly felt happy and ready for anything. He was whistling softly by the time they reached the jackpine clearing and took the last turn down to the Fort.

4 · *Preparation for Battle*

But William Henry was not prepared for what he found inside Fort Pitt. Almost everything he saw both surprised and bewildered him. The Fort itself—a square log stockade, with thick turrets for howitzers and cannon—was more or less what he expected. But the soldiers were not. He had never seen soldiers like these. They seemed to slouch about and to care little for discipline or anything else. William Henry hadn't had a proper salute since he arrived, except from the commanding officer.

The soldiers here were more like frontiersmen, or at least what Ensign Harrison imagined frontiersmen were like. Scarcely any officers or privates wore proper military hats. They went about in fox or coonskin caps or homespun turbans. Some even went bareheaded. And there were no thick boots, like the ones William Henry wore. Here the men all seemed to prefer Indian moccasins. Their shirts, too, were different—mostly of deerskin and very long, falling like skirts to their knees. Their breeches were of stout rawhide leather, but they were dirty and covered with animal grease.

Even their fighting equipment was strange. True, they carried rifles and muskets, and all had proper powderhorns and bullet pouches. But the muskets were generally the old-style Kentucky ones, six-feet long. And it was odd, too, to see a tomahawk and a long, shiny hunting knife tucked in each belt. What were the men trying to look like? Indians?

Then there was the "game bag," a small pouch with thong harness that William Henry saw slung across every shoulder. The game bag was supposed to carry all personal food supplies. But how could it? It was so small a hungry man couldn't put one supper in it. To satisfy his curiosity, William Henry examined one thoroughly the first chance he got. All he found inside the game bag were a few handfuls of parched corn, several strips of dry, jerked deer meat, and a small flagon of brandy. How could men fight a war on food like that? And how could they go about dressed as they did and call themselves soldiers? Everything he saw during his first days at the garrison shook his confidence.

But he felt better when he inspected the artillery. The cannon were all in good shape—the powder and tinderboxes dry, the metal balls neatly stacked, and the wide-mouth gun barrels free of smoke and rust. And the posted guards at the stockade's corners were pacing back and forth, always on duty.

Yet when the men were off duty, William Henry heard them grumble about the food and pay, about the right way to fight Indians, about the government in Philadelphia, and argue loudly that "only fools would stay in the army in this forsaken wilderness." Some men even talked openly of desertion. William Henry was horrified. He wondered what President Washington would say about soldiers who talked like this.

During his fourth day at the Fort, William Henry passed a grizzled-looking soldier sitting on a stump outside the gates. The man did not salute him or even look up, so William Henry stopped. The soldier still took no notice of him, but went on oiling a battered-looking flintlock that seemed fully to engage his slow, lazy attention. He was rubbing the flintlock with bear's grease, turning it over and over in his hand gently, as if he held a treasure. Yet William Henry could plainly see that the barrel of the musket was badly bent, and seemed to have had no better care than the soldier himself. Irritated, he came nearer.

"How can you hit anything with that old bent musket?" William Henry asked, an edge in his voice.

The grizzled soldier stopped and looked up at him a moment with an amused expression on his face, then went on slowly greasing the gun. William Henry was about to repeat his question when the soldier suddenly asked, "Whar ye hail from, youngun?"

"Virginia," William Henry said through tight lips.

"Kinda new out here, ain't ye—jedgin' from yer get-up?"

"I've been training in Philadelphia," William Henry said, trying to put some weight and dignity into his voice.

The soldier did not respond to this immediately. Finally he grunted and nodded his head. "Philadelphia. Wal, I declare. So thet's whar all you bright-faced fellers is from!" He wiped his mouth with his dirty jacket, then leaned back. "Never been to Philadelphia. Never goin', neither. Cain't stand the thought of this'n and that'n bumpin' you around in the streets." He fell silent again. Then he took up the gun and squinted down the crooked barrel. "You wuz askin' about this here gun. Old Daisy, I calls her." He looked hard at the weapon now, as if studying it. "I'll tell yer, youngun, there's them what thinks Old Daisy ain't too dependable." Here he stopped and patted the gun affectionately. "But most of the fellers what thought so—includin' some redskins—ain't around eny more to talk about it."

Having delivered this remark with a lazy drawl, the

grizzled soldier cleared his throat emphatically and spat noisily onto the frosty ground. Finally he raised a weather-beaten hand and pointed into the distance. " 'Pears to me thet fer the edjication of the young I'd better illustrate somethin' of what I'm sayin'. See that thar loose peg a-stickin' out the right-hand gate of the Fort?"

William Henry nodded, then smiled. The peg was a good thirty yards away and only about an inch and a half in diameter. In fact, he had to look hard to be able to see it.

Without speaking again the grizzled soldier, with what seemed like one movement, tilted his gun, rammed in powder and ball, snapped the weapon to his shoulder and, without seeming to aim, pulled the trigger. William Henry ran over to see the result. To his amazement, he found the wooden peg driven hard into the gate of the stockade. He hurried back to the soldier.

"You hit it!" he exclaimed.

"Um, I was aimin' to," the soldier admitted calmly as he ran the ramrod through the barrel of his smoking gun. "Always did hate to see a loose peg." Then he looked up at William Henry again, his blue eyes twinkling. "Does that answer yer question about Old Daisy?"

"Yes," William Henry acknowledged quickly. "Yes sir, it does." He turned to leave, then swung back. "I shouldn't have said anything about your musket," he said apologetically. "I reckon I was just judging by appearances."

Something about the sincerity in the tall, serious-faced young Ensign must have caught the grizzled soldier's fancy, for when he spoke again his voice was warm with good nature.

"No harm, youngun," he commented. "If ye don't ask nuthin' in this world, ye don't find out nuthin'."

William Henry nodded, smiled, and walked away. He felt considerably humbled by his exchange with the soldier.

In the busy days that followed, William Henry's opinion of the Fort and its men slowly began to change. He became happier and more interested in his daily duties. For one thing, he made friends with three young lieutenants—John Whistler, Meriwether Lewis, and

And without seeming to aim, he pulled the trigger.

William Clark. They were getting their first instruction in Indian warfare, too. The veterans who taught them seemed to know their business, even though most of them, at first glance, looked rather unimpressive, like the grizzled old soldier with the bent musket.

"We're getting to be more like Indians every day," Meriwether Lewis observed, as he practiced hurling his new tomahawk at an oak tree.

"We've tried everything except how to give a war whoop," William Henry agreed, grinning. "By nighttime I'm so tired I couldn't give a whoop if I knew how."

Certainly they had drilled hard. Their day began with a blaring bugle call at five in the morning and ended long after dusk. But how many things they had learned! It was not easy to remember everything.

William Henry and the other young officers had been shown how troops should be scattered through the forest to avoid flanking attacks by the enemies, how to place a camp to avoid ambush, how sentries should be posted to the best advantage, and when not to make a campfire.

As they took daily journeys through the wilderness around Fort Pitt, they also learned how to notch a trail, how to shoot from trees the way the Indians did, and how to step when marching in the exact footprints of the man ahead, so that an Indian scout could never count the size of the regiment. They were instructed in close fighting with the bayonet. They also saw now the advantages of carrying a knife and tomahawk in case their guns failed. And finally, they learned how to raft heavy cannon over streams and marshes, and how to lay a road where there was no road.

All this careful training fascinated William Henry, and he learned quickly. Yet he grew impatient to put his training into practice. When the order finally came to proceed to Fort Washington, he was overjoyed.

5 · *On to Fort Washington*

William Henry's regiment floated slowly down the Ohio River on broad flatboats, headed for Fort Washington and the Northwest Territory. The flatboats carried passengers and freight of all kinds, and had to be poled along by hand by strong rivermen who tugged and sweated night and day.

The soldiers were accompanied downriver by several pioneer families. These pioneers had brought along their domestic animals—cows, hogs, chickens, oxen, dogs, cats—and every kind of personal belonging, as there were few stores in the new country. One small girl even carried a screeching parrot which she never let out of her sight.

"What's your parrot's name?" William Henry asked once, poking his finger into the cage.

"Gabby," the girl said. "Because he talks so much." Then she touched William Henry's arm. "Mister soldier," she said, "you'd better watch your finger. Gabby always nips strangers when he can. Don't you, Gabby?" The parrot blinked and nodded. The small girl seemed pleased and ran happily back to her parents, swinging the cage on her arm.

William Henry turned away and stared out moodily at the sluggish river. The flatboat moved so slowly he felt that he might be an old man before he got to Fort Washington. The boat was heavily laden, the deck covered with great wooden barrels and kegs of salt, sugar, spices, rum, gunpowder, iron filings and sorghum molasses, all bound downriver to scattered ports as far as St. Louis and even New Orleans. In Virginia, William Henry had always traveled by fast stagecoaches drawn by four horses, or else by canal boats pulled along by horses on a towpath by the water's edge. This crawling pace downriver was getting on his nerves.

The first sight of Fort Washington, however, raised his spirits. At a distance the fort looked very much like Fort Pitt, only there seemed to be more activity on the shore. As the flatboat put in, William Henry saw other boats being hastily loaded and shoved off, some upriver, some downriver. He saw soldiers running back and forth, too. But why were so many of them without guns, he wondered. Some of the soldiers lay sprawled on the wharf, exhausted, almost unable to move.

When William Henry leaped ashore and beckoned his men to follow, a tired-looking soldier on the wharf shouted, "Too late, friends!"

"Why? What's happened?" William Henry asked, as the people on shore crowded around the newcomers.

"Indians. We got licked four days ago. Worst lickin' we ever had on the frontier! Lost half of our men. General St. Clair was bad hit, too. Most everyone's pullin' up stakes afore we all lose our scalps! You boys better head back yourselves."

William Henry paled but his jaw tightened. He

turned to his men. Some of them looked worried and undecided. "We're not heading back," William Henry said firmly. "My orders are to report to General St. Clair. Follow me, men." With that, he marched his men toward the Fort.

It was a grim welcome for the new recruits, but they soon pitched in to try and restore order and confidence to the fort and the surrounding settlement. William Henry's outward calmness continued to give courage to his men. Even General St. Clair was happy to see him, though the General, as he recovered from his wounds, muttered something about "these beardless youngsters the government is sending west!"

But after a few weeks General St. Clair said no more about "beardless youngsters." William Henry and his men worked like beavers. All that winter they were on the alert: drilling, inspecting the guns, getting the new supplies distributed. Everyone expected the Indians to come down from the north at any time and raid Fort Washington. The garrison had to be prepared for any emergency. The settlers moved their wives and children

The first sight of Fort Washington raised his spirits.

into the stockade for safety. The sentries were doubled. Scouts were sent north in parties of three to try to determine the next move of the Indians.

In the meantime, messengers were dispatched to Philadelphia to carry the news of General St. Clair's disastrous defeat to President Washington.

On hearing the report, the President acted immediately. He called for more volunteers to increase the army, and asked General "Mad" Anthony Wayne, who had earned his nickname as a hero in the Revolution, to come from retirement and take command of the national army.

General Wayne hurried to Fort Pitt in the spring of 1792 to train more recruits. Among those called back to Fort Pitt to help in this program was Ensign Harrison. Wayne was so impressed by the young Ensign's attention to his duties that he promoted him to lieutenant and made him one of his aides-de-camp. This meant that William Henry had to stay by General Wayne's side, at headquarters or in battle, ready to dispatch orders or to carry out any personal or military service for the commander.

When General Wayne felt that his new army was prepared for battle, the troops moved once again to Fort Washington. At this point, Lieutenant Harrison took the army pay he had saved and bought a horse. He had to have a horse if he was to carry out the General's orders swiftly. As the army did not provide horses, he had to buy one himself. The horse he chose was a high-spirited stallion, and he bought it for sixty dollars from a discouraged pioneer who was returning east. After he had ridden the stallion a few days and had seen how quickly he responded to the rein and how sure-footedly he galloped down the forest trails, he named him Fear-naught.

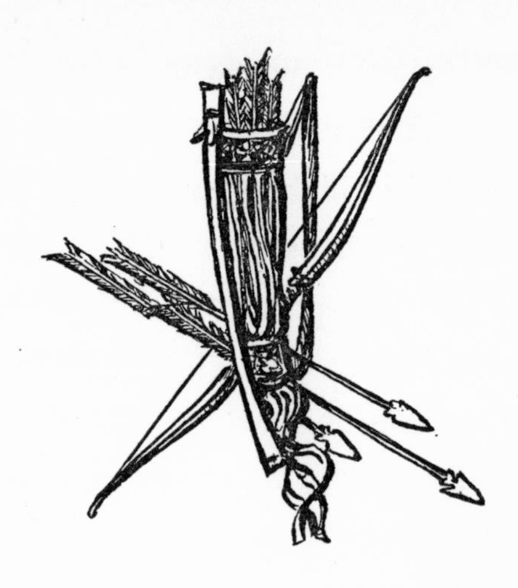

6 · *Marching Toward Indians*

General Wayne, his dark old eyes flashing, addressed his young officers in the autumn of 1793.

"Gentlemen, we must show our strength at once, or lose the Northwest Territory to the Indians and British." He paused, eying the serious faces before him, letting his words sink in. "As President Washington used to say, 'Don't let the enemy surprise *you.* Act first. Surprise *him.*' " He waited again, watching his men. "If that's good advice, gentlemen, with respect to

Redcoats, it's twice as good with Indians. Their technique in war is always surprise and ambush."

He strode to the chinked wall behind his desk and with one finger traced an area on the large map that hung there. "At present we have three forts. These forts lie directly north of us. Fort Hamilton, Fort St. Clair, Fort Jefferson. They form our only line of defense. Beyond Fort Jefferson we have nothing." He stopped then, as if lost in thought.

Lieutenant Harrison stepped forward. Later he wondered at his boldness. "Sir, may I offer a suggestion?"

General Wayne did not answer immediately, but finally he looked up. "Yes, Lieutenant?"

"With a detachment of men I could go forward and start building another fort, sir."

This time the tense, lined face of the General relaxed and he smiled. "Precisely what was in my mind, Lieutenant. I'm pleased that you volunteered the idea before I spoke." He turned to the map again, studying it. "In fact, Lieutenant, we want two forts. One here. One here." He indicated positions about halfway into the Territory, along the line that would one day divide the states of Ohio and Indiana.

"I'm pleased you volunteered the idea before I spoke."

So it was that later that winter and all the next spring Lieutenant Harrison directed work on the new forts, under the able eyes of Major Burbeck and General Wayne. One post became Fort Greenville (erected on the site of present-day Greenville, Ohio) and the other Fort Recovery (east of where Portland, Indiana now stands).

Young Lieutenant Harrison knew little about the building of forts but he wisely chose men from his regiment who at least had had experience in building log cabins. Even so, it was slow and bitter labor. And it was dangerous as well. All the time the soldiers worked, hewing the heavy hickory and oak timbers, and dragging them through the swampy bottomlands, they felt the watching eyes of the Indians on them. It was bad enough to have to hack and chop through thickets of cane and tangles of blackberry, without wondering when an Indian arrow would strike through the sunless forest.

Yet the soldiers worked on feverishly each day, and at night slept uneasily with their loaded muskets and rifles locked in their arms. By May, 1794, the two new forts were completed and stocked with ammunition and supplies sent forward hurriedly from Fort Washington.

The following month a small band of Indians attacked Fort Recovery. But they did not attack in force, nor did they pursue the attack for very long. Obviously this roving band was only testing the strength of the new position, for after three days the rattle of arrows against the stout logs suddenly stopped and the Indians melted into the forest as quietly as they had come.

Lieutenant Harrison wondered if General Wayne would take this small attack as a warning. The General did. He ordered his army to march north in pursuit, and when his men reached the Maumee River, he gave the command to erect still another fort. This one was to be named Fort Defiance.

While the new fort was being completed, General Wayne asked for two scouting parties to locate the enemy and to collect all available information about their activities. One party, led by Captain DeButts, was to go upstream along the winding Maumee River. Lieutenant Harrison was instructed to direct the second party, and to lead it downstream where the roving Shawnees were thought to be.

Both scouting parties were to carry flags of truce and gifts for any Indian chiefs encountered who were not openly hostile. Lieutenant Harrison, less experienced than Captain DeButts, was given the best Indian scout and guide to accompany him. This was a half-white, half-Indian named Walli. Walli knew every inch of the surrounding country as well as the habits and languages of the principal tribes. He was invaluable, as Lieutenant Harrison reported months later when he wrote down his experiences among the Indian tribes of the Northwest Territory.

7 · *The Scouting Trip*

The scouting parties started through the forest at dawn the next day.

Indeed Lieutenant Harrison had reason to be grateful for having such an experienced guide as Walli to aid him on his first scouting trip. Without Walli he would have had to rely solely on a rough map and luck to locate the hidden Indian villages downstream.

The first eight hours passed without incident. But late in the afternoon Lieutenant Harrison and his men sighted a young Indian boy along the river bank. He was making a canoe, and as the men came nearer they saw that he was wetting and flattening some long strips of bark to stretch over the stout braces of white cedar which would support the light finished craft. When the young Indian turned and saw them, he leaped up and scurried into the forest, leaving his unassembled canoe where it was.

From this incident the men judged they were nearing an Indian village, or at least an encampment. Lieutenant Harrison gave the order to proceed cautiously. Walli then suggested that the scouting party go to a rocky promontory near by which afforded an excellent view of the surrounding country. Lieutenant Harrison agreed.

When they reached the high limestone ledge, Walli shinnied up a large elm, shaded his eyes, and looked searchingly in all four directions. Suddenly he let out a soft cry and slid back to the ground.

"Shawnee camp," he said, looking pleased. "About two miles."

This was good luck indeed. The Shawnees were one of the tribes that General Wayne was most eager to know about. They were a large tribe who had originally lived on the banks of the Scioto River just north of the Ohio. But now they were apparently on the move. Were they on the warpath? This was what Lieutenant Harrison had been ordered to find out.

General Wayne had told him that the Shawnees had two chiefs who were twin brothers. One brother was Olliwachi, known as the Prophet because of his magical powers as a medicine man. The Prophet was said always to carry a beaded bag made from the skin of a white wolf. The bag was filled with herbs, rare plants, and the bones of animals which gave him and his tribe great powers. This chief was known to be very warlike and full of hatred toward the white settlers.

But it was the Prophet's brother, Tecumseh, who most interested Lieutenant Harrison. He was said to be only nineteen years old and already a great warrior and hunter. According to Walli, Tecumseh had passed his severe tribal test as a warrior when he was sixteen. This meant that he had skillfully fashioned his own hickory bow and arrow, made his own war club of deerhorn, daubed his face suitably with ocher and blackberry juice, shaved his long black hair with a fine-edged shell into a warrior's topknot, stuck the brightest colored feathers into his headband, and caught the weasel tails for his beaded moccasins.

It meant he had done harder things, too. He had held hot stones in his hands without crying out in pain. He had lived in the forest for one moon's time without weapons, with only the food that he could snare or catch with his own hands. He had brought in the scalp of an enemy and fastened it to the leather door-flap of his hut. And, along the banks of the Ohio River, he had twice raided the flatboats bringing the white settlers into the West.

Tecumseh—or "Shooting Star," as the name translates from the Shawnee language—was described by veteran soldiers at the fort as tall, handsome, and exceptionally strong, with dark, piercing eyes and a lively intelligence. He was reported to be a fine orator, and persuasive in argument both with his own tribe and the chiefs of neighboring tribes.

It had been rumored for some time around the American army headquarters that Tecumseh was working for an Indian confederation, an organization of all the tribes throughout the vast area of 250,000 square miles of the Northwest Territory who could be brought together to resist the white settlers. Consequently, it was most important that Lieutenant Harrison discover Tecumseh's plans.

The scouting party approached the Shawnee camp at dusk. There was great activity. A huge fire was burning, drums were beating, and a tall masked figure was dancing and wailing before the assembled warriors. It was obvious that something of importance was taking place. Walli told Lieutenant Harrison, as they crept nearer, that the masked figure was the Prophet.

It was decided that Walli would enter the Indian camp alone, under the pretext of being a wandering hunter in search of shelter. When he had gathered what information he could, he would slip out of the camp under cover of darkness and report back to the scouting party who would lie waiting and hidden in the forest.

Walli was gone an hour. It seemed like a day to Lieutenant Harrison and his party, crouched in the mosquito-infested thicket. The Indian campfire blazed higher and higher as they waited. The mounting light revealed the outline of the whole camp, a large circle of small round huts. The Shawnees did not use teepees for shelter. Instead, they stuck poles into the ground in a circle, then bent the poles together and tied them at one end. They covered these frames with mats of reeds and rushes, and the skins of animals after the hides had been stretched and tanned.

Lieutenant Harrison, as he watched the dancing Prophet and the painted faces of the warriors, felt a thrust of fear. The warriors, wearing only breech-clouts and buckskin moccasins, looked sinister in the unsteady light. What if they should not believe Walli? What if they recognized him as a spy?

The voice of the Prophet was getting louder. Now he was shaking a gourd medicine-rattle filled with stones, and stamping the ground as he went on wailing.

When Walli finally returned he looked grave. "The Prophet is 'making medicine,' " Walli said. "He is calling on the spirits of nature to protect the Shawnees against the coming of the Long Knives." (The Indians always called the white men "Long Knives" because of their sabers and long swords.)

"Was Tecumseh there?" Lieutenant Harrison asked.

"No," Walli answered. "They say Tecumseh has been gone many moons on a long journey. He has gone to see the great chiefs of the other tribes—the Miamis, Wabashis, Kickapoos, Piankeshaws, Mascouten, Potawatami, Wyandots, and Delawares. He is now at the camp of Little Turtle, the Miami."

Lieutenant Harrison frowned. Little Turtle was the warlike chief who only a short time before had attacked and defeated Colonel Hardin and the Kentucky militia, taking one hundred and fifty scalps.

"What is the Prophet saying to them?" Lieutenant Harrison asked Walli.

"He is saying the Long Knives must be driven from the Shawnee hunting grounds," Walli answered. "The deer of the forest and the fish of the rivers belong to the Indian. He is working the tribe up for war. When I was there he was full of threats. 'We will cut the Long Knives down like the tall grasses!' he said. 'The poles of our huts will be heavy with their scalps before many moons have sailed the sky! The flames of their cabins and their burning bones will brighten our campfire, O brothers! And only the wolves and fox will prowl where they have been!' "

It was obvious from this report that the Shawnees were preparing for battle. But why was Tecumseh at

The warriors looked sinister in the unsteady light.

the camp of Little Turtle? It seemed unlikely that the tribe would go to war with one of their chiefs absent.

Lieutenant Harrison decided to go north to the Miami camp in the hope of finding out what Tecumseh and Little Turtle were discussing. If the Miami were also preparing for war he would then hurry back and warn General Wayne that there was a general uprising among the Indians.

The scouting party pushed on that night and made camp about three miles north of the Shawnee settlement. They slept in the open under buffalo robes, ate cold food, and denied themselves a campfire. They posted a sentry and lay down with their muskets at their sides.

8 · *At Little Turtle's Camp*

The next morning the scouting party struck out due north, toward the hunting lands of the Miami at the headwaters of the Maumee River. When the trails disappeared they cut their way with hunting knife, ax, and saber through tangles of sassafras and swamproot. Their progress was difficult. The wind blew hard out of the north and the sky was a ceiling of slate-gray, making the forest dim even in daylight.

Lieutenant Harrison had decided to use his flag of

truce in an attempt to enter peaceably into the Miami camp. The Indians did not always recognize the white flag, and frequently took gestures of this kind to be a show of weakness. If Little Turtle should happen to feel this way, the scouting party would all be taken captive. It was a chance the Lieutenant had decided to take.

When, in the late afternoon, the party entered the vast circle of painted teepees that made up the Miami camp, they were relieved to find that Little Turtle himself came forward and welcomed them warmly. He at once ordered his squaws to leave his teepee—a sign of respect to his guests.

Little Turtle was forty-nine years old at this time, but still exceptionally vigorous. He wore a great jangling mass of jewelry on his arms and legs, and his painted body had all the colors of a rainbow. On his head was a large square hat which he kept re-arranging. He was a loud talker, smiled more than most Indians, and seemed at ease with his white visitors.

No sooner were his guests seated than he brought out an enormous stone-bowled peace pipe, with a draped fringe of eagle feathers, and offered it first to Lieutenant

Harrison. The Lieutenant took a puff and passed the pipe along the line, as was customary.

While this ceremony was taking place, Little Turtle, with a great air of both pride and secrecy, strode to the back of his lodge and, from beneath a buffalo robe, drew out a large earthen jug. He raised the jug, drank deeply from it with an air of satisfaction, and then offered it to Lieutenant Harrison.

"Drink!" Little Turtle commanded. "It is your Long Knife drink. It is powerful medicine. Good. Good."

Lieutenant Harrison hesitated, then tilted the jug and took a small swallow. The raw liquor burned his throat, but he managed to keep from gasping aloud, even as tears sprang to his eyes. When he saw Little Turtle watching him, he covered his face with his hands in an attempt to stifle the cough that rose in his throat.

Little Turtle took the jug from him and passed it next to a tall young Indian seated near him who, with arms folded, had been quietly watching the white visitors.

"Tecumseh, you drink?" Little Turtle asked.

Lieutenant Harrison looked up quickly. So this dignified, handsome young warrior was the famous Tecumseh!

Tecumseh spoke for the first time. "No," he said flatly. "I do not drink the water that tastes like fire. It is the drink of the Long Knives. But it makes our Indian brothers stagger like crazy buffalo."

Little Turtle frowned and looked thoughtful, but Lieutenant Harrison noticed that he took another long pull at the jug before returning it to its hiding place under the buffalo rug. Tecumseh still did not move, but his eyes never left the visitors. He seemed to be studying them as if they were curious animals.

Unlike Little Turtle, Tecumseh wore no jewelry except for one great stone locket around his neck. His face and body were unpainted. A single eagle feather stood up straight from the headband around his long black hair.

In this interval of silence Lieutenant Harrison had a chance to observe the teepee. He knew that Little Turtle was a great trader with the British and French and loved the many strange articles from the white man's world. The teepee was filled with steel axes, the blades greased and polished. There were huge kettles of copper stacked near the entrance, a hollowed log full of shiny muskets, bolts of bright-colored cloth, and a reed basket overflowing with beads and buttons of all size and description.

"Little Turtle, great chief of the Miami," Lieutenant Harrison finally said, using Walli as interpreter, "do you not fear making war on the Long Knives?"

The Chief was slow to answer. He folded his arms, frowned, and then faced the scouting party, pounding his bare chest until it thudded like a war drum. Finally he shouted, "Little Turtle fears no man, be his skin of copper or the whiteness of rain!"

Tecumseh nodded gravely, in acceptance of this proud boast. He puffed at the peace pipe, curling gray rings into the still air.

When a few moments passed and Little Turtle did not continue, Lieutenant Harrison spoke up again, Walli translating quickly. "Great Chief, your courage no warrior can question. You have fought many battles. The ridge-pole of your lodge is heavy with scalps. But why must you fight your white brothers who wish to live beside you in peace?"

He hesitated, and Chief Little Turtle wagged his hand, adjusted his square hat, then signaled to Tecumseh, who suddenly rose and spoke. "Long Knife," Tecumseh said, "will there not come a time when the cabins of the white settlers will be spread over our lands like a buffalo robe? Oh, this can happen, warrior of the palefaces! It can happen unless all the Red Men between the Great Waters join in battle against you. I see this written in the sky. I hear this message whispering from the night grasses. And my brother, the great Prophet of the Shawnee, speaks of it always, and always with fear and a heavy heart. What shall be done to make the Indian walk without fear toward the future?"

Little Turtle stared straight ahead, his plucked eyebrows pulled down in thought as Tecumseh finished. Then, after several moments of silence, he spoke. "My great brother, Shooting Star of the Shawnees, speaks easily. His words ripple as the fresh brook runs after rain. And with wisdom he speaks, as a chief. But he carries fear in his heart. Little Turtle does not fear. Little Turtle has behind him the power of the Redcoat Long Knives. He does not run and tremble before the fair-haired men from the East, though they come like leaves

The three chieftains.

in autumn. He stands alone. He does not need the power of the Shawnee, or the Kickapoo, or any of his Red brothers. If battles come in the future, he will meet the Long Knives alone."

With that, he waved pointedly toward the scalps dangling and drying on the pole behind him, sat down stiffly and folded his arms again.

Lieutenant Harrison waited. When Little Turtle said no more, Lieutenant Harrison spoke earnestly. As he reported later, he tried to assure Little Turtle and Tecumseh that the American settlers did not wish war, that they did not wish to take any Indian lands for which they did not pay, and that they hoped to live in peace beside their Indian brothers. But he added that the Great White Father, President Washington, was troubled and angered by the border massacres committed by the Indians, and that these acts of violence must stop.

Again there was a long silence when he had finished. Lieutenant Harrison waited for Little Turtle and Tecumseh to reply. When it became obvious that the grave faces before him had no intention of answering him, he rose, bowed, signaled to his party, and left the lodge. Once outside he conferred quickly with Walli. Walli was of the opinion that Little Turtle had spoken his mind and there was nothing that would make him change it. As for Tecumseh, Walli admitted that it was difficult to interpret the thoughts that lay behind his dignified and silent countenance.

As they headed for the forest Lieutenant Harrison took one last look at the Indian camp. He saw that the warriors were all in full war-paint. The best thing he could do, he quickly decided, was to hurry back to General Wayne and warn him that the Shawnee and Miami chiefs were clearly prepared to resist the American army.

"Ah, Little Turtle and Tecumseh," General Wayne murmured with satisfaction when Lieutenant Harrison reported to him. "They're the ones we're after. We've a particular score to settle with Little Turtle. He has massacred hundreds of settlers. How many warriors, Lieutenant, do you estimate that he has?"

"Possibly a thousand, sir," Lieutenant Harrison answered.

"Any evidence of British militia?" the General wanted to know.

"No, sir."

"Were the Indians in war dress?"

"Yes, sir. In full paint and war dress. The first night out we saw a war dance in the Shawnee camp. I think they're worked up for a fight, sir," Lieutenant Harrison said. "Walli agrees."

General Wayne looked grave. He paced the fort's puncheon floor as Lieutenant Harrison waited eagerly for his decision. He did not have to wait long.

"Then the Indians expect us," General Wayne said. "Good! They will not be disappointed. Their main fighting force, Lieutenant, is obviously at the Miami camp. We'll strike there first. Sound the drums and bugles. Carry the word to all officers and men. We march at dawn."

9 · *Battle of Fallen Timbers*

The march downstream, made in hot weather, was miserable. It was August now, and in the swampy bottomlands the mosquitoes and flies attacked at their worst. There was a steady *slap-slap* as the soldiers swatted the pesky insects forever buzzing around their faces.

Lieutenant Harrison was riding his horse Fearnaught, and staying close to General Wayne, ready to dispatch any sudden order. He looked down with pride at the green ribbon pinned diagonally across his chest. In preparation for the coming battle General Wayne had given each of his three aides-de-camp a ribbon to designate their authority.

At the top of a low hill Lieutenant Harrison suddenly plucked at the General's sleeve. "Sir, do you see where those giant trees are? The fallen ones—about a mile forward?"

General Wayne nodded.

"Our scout says they were toppled by a recent hurricane in these parts. Do you think, sir, the Indians might be waiting for us behind those fallen timbers?"

"Possibly. Very possibly. It's a likely place for them." The General reined in his horse, then turned to Brigadier General Wilkinson and Colonel Hamtranck who were close behind. "We will divide our forces here. Scatter your men out, right and left. Have them fix bayonets and proceed cautiously, keeping within sight of each other until we reach those fallen trees just ahead."

The orders were carried out and the men advanced slowly, half-crouched, alert to every sound from the woods ahead. Suddenly a shot rang out, cutting through the leaves above General Wayne's head. Then, as quickly, came the bloodcurdling war whoop of the savages. Arrows and bullets began to rain down on the advancing soldiers. The battle had begun.

For an hour the struggle raged, as the two forces kept under cover and exchanged a furious musket fire. With each minute, General Wayne's forces crept nearer, foot by foot, toward the enemy who lay concealed beyond the great fallen timbers. The soldiers were formed now in a wide semi-circle in the hope of closing in gradually on the Indian forces.

Suddenly General Wayne shouted to Lieutenant Harrison, "Fix bayonets! Charge!"

Lieutenant Harrison galloped right and left across the searing line of fire to carry the orders to the men fighting on the flanks of the battle line. He bent low over Fearnaught as the horse leaped over logs and plunged recklessly through the sticky brambles with his young rider. With the arrows whizzing around him, Lieutenant Harrison felt strangely calm. An hour before, when the battle had not yet started, he had felt his hands trembling on the bridle reins. But now that the fight was on he felt nothing but a kind of wild courage.

With fixed bayonets the soldiers ran forward, shouting now like Indians themselves. A tomahawk grazed Lieutenant Harrison's ear and stuck deep into a tree behind him. The savages were revealing themselves now, standing up, their hunting knives gleaming in their hands as they awaited the oncoming rush of the soldiers. Lieutenant Harrison saw the flash of a Redcoat in the shadows. So the British militia were in the fight, too!

The hand-to-hand fighting had begun. Indians were tumbling from the trees now and swinging down on grapevines. Knots of squirming, struggling, grappling figures rolled and tumbled and grunted as the desperate fight went on. Lieutenant Harrison was everywhere, urging his men forward, swinging his saber and slashing at the painted bodies that tried to wrench him from his saddle.

How long the fight went on he could not have said. But suddenly the Indians, as if in answer to some mysterious signal, turned and fled into the forest—their wild, fearful wails echoing through the trees.

The American forces pursued them without letup, the men stopping only to drop to one knee and reload before running on again. The Indians fell back as far as

The hand-to-hand fighting had begun.

the British fort, only to find the gates closed in their faces. Howling against this betrayal by their white allies, they fled on downriver.

General Wayne led his victorious forces straight to the gates of the British fort. He was tempted to fire on it, too. But he knew such action might start a war with England, so he withdrew and camped that night within shooting range of the enemy garrison.

When the results of the battle were known, the American forces had lost 31 men, with 102 wounded. The Indians and British had lost close to 500. It was a great victory for the Americans, for the Indians had put their greatest warriors into the battle.

History has recorded that more than a thousand Indians fought at the Battle of Fallen Timbers. Not only were Little Turtle and his men there, but also young Tecumseh of the Shawnee tribe. And Chief Buckongahelas, the Delaware; Tarhe, of the Wyandot tribe; and Turkeyfoot of the Ottawas.

In his dispatch the next day to President Washington, giving an account of the victory, General Wayne added:

"The bravery and conduct of every officer belonging to the army, from the generals down to the ensigns, merit my highest praise. There were, however, some whose range and situation placed their conduct in a very conspicuous point of view, and which I observed with pleasure and most lively gratitude; among whom I beg leave to mention Brigadier General Wilkinson, and Colonel Hamtranck, the commandant of the right and left wings of the legion, whose brave example inspired the troops; and to these I must add the names of my faithful and gallant aides-de-camp Captains DeButts and T. Lewis, and Lieutenant Harrison who, with Adjutant General Major Mills, rendered the most essential service by communicating my orders in every direction, and by their conduct and bravery exciting the troops to press for victory."

When Lieutenant Harrison heard that his name had been mentioned in the dispatch to the President, he was of course greatly pleased.

"I don't know what I did to deserve it," he remarked later to Captain DeButts, as they rode back toward Fort Defiance. "But it certainly was a good battle. I declare, if I hadn't been so busy with the General's orders, I would have been too frightened to lift my saber."

He patted Fearnaught's glossy neck. "Too bad Fearnaught didn't get a medal," he said. "He saved my life several times that day. Hear that, Fearnaught? Hear it, old fellow?" Fearnaught neighed immediately in answer. Apparently he had both heard and understood.

The rest of that fall and winter Lieutenant Harrison served General Wayne back at Fort Greenville. There was much to do now in keeping the string of new forts supplied with men and ammunition. Although the surrounding Indian tribes were causing no new trouble after their defeat at Fallen Timbers, General Wayne felt that steps should be taken to guarantee future peace with them. He dispatched messengers to the tribal chiefs, inviting them all to a great peace council to be held at Fort Greenville in the summer of 1795.

When the chiefs accepted, even General Wayne was greatly relieved. He showed this by permitting several of his younger officers a leave of absence from their duties. This was something he rarely did, for he was a stickler for discipline and worked his men hard.

"Pray return here in three weeks," he said to the young officers, and then gave one of his rare, twisted smiles as he added, "and come back in one piece. Don't get into any mischief or wrestling matches with the flatboaters. They're half-horse and half-alligator, those rivermen." He straightened and saluted them all. "Fare ye well, gentlemen."

The young officers returned the salute and hurried to their horses.

10 · *A Treaty and a Girl*

Lieutenant Harrison had decided to spend his welcome holiday in Kentucky with some friends who had written to say they had moved west. So he headed south, eager now to get away for a while from the confining routine of life in a wilderness fort. He had no particular plans except to have some fun and perhaps find time to explore idly the pioneer settlements on the river.

Certainly he had not counted on meeting Anna Symmes, the beautiful daughter of Judge John Cleves

Symmes. The Symmes family had just come west and were building a new house at North Bend, near Fort Washington.

Lieutenant Harrison happened to be on the wharf the day Anna came visiting at the Fort. He was watching the sights in the busy river-town as he waited for the blacksmith to finish shoeing Fearnaught. As a matter of fact, he had his mouth full of maple-sugar candy when he first saw Anna Symmes. She was getting off a flatboat. For a moment, Lieutenant Harrison stopped chewing the candy and watched her. It was many months since he had seen a white woman his own age, and the one he was staring at seemed prettier than any he had ever seen, even in Philadelphia. But who was she? How was he ever to find out?

When she walked past him, he tried to catch her eye. He even raised his cap. But if Anna Symmes saw the staring handsome young Lieutenant, she made no sign. Lieutenant Harrison took a few steps after her toward the Fort, then stopped. But he watched her until she disappeared from sight.

That night there was a dance at the Fort for the officers. The female guests were practically all the ladies from the surrounding settlement who could walk—young and old, ugly and beautiful, married and unmarried. The officers were starved for feminine company and had sent out general invitations to every house.

Lieutenant Harrison appeared at the dance early. The first polka had not even been called, but already his eyes were searching the large room. What luck! There was the beautiful girl he had seen earlier in the day, and she was talking to his friend Meriwether Lewis. He greeted Meriwether cordially, very cordially. And then he was introduced to Anna. Ten minutes later they were dancing. An hour later they were walking under the spring moon and talking like old friends.

When they parted that evening, Lieutenant Harrison left with the promise that he could visit Anna Symmes in her new home when next he came south. He told her eagerly that he would come south again when he had finished helping General Wayne at the Indian council. Anna teased him and said he would probably end up with an Indian girl, as did so many soldiers. Lieutenant Harrison denied any interest in Indian girls. In fact, he told Anna he had never met a girl anywhere, anytime, like her. She laughed then, and let him hold her hand an extra long moment when he bowed and said good-bye.

Though he hated to leave Fort Washington, Lieutenant Harrison was curious to meet, face to face, the Indians who had been invited to Fort Greenville for the peace council.

When he got back to General Wayne's headquarters, more than eleven hundred chiefs and warriors from the various tribes were gathered there, among them Little Turtle. Of the principal tribes of the region, the Shawnees were the only Indians not represented. They had lost many warriors in the Battle of Fallen Timbers, and Tecumseh vowed vengeance. He refused any talk of peace.

In fact, encouraged by his brother, the Prophet, Tecumseh called on all his warriors to return to their Indian ways. He would tolerate no one in his tribe who wore the white man's dress, who ate the white man's food, or tasted the white man's firewater. For a while he even forbade the use of muskets in his tribe, insisting that the Indians' weapons should be only the tomahawk and bow and arrow.

But the tribes that sat down with General Wayne and his officers at Fort Greenville were more than ready to discuss peace. Deserted by the British and sorely defeated by the Americans, they knew they must strike a bargain or face again the fury of "the-General-who-never-sleeps"—their name now for General Wayne.

Lieutenant Harrison watched with care how General Wayne handled the Indians. For an impatient man, the General seemed almost tediously patient. The hours stretched into days and the days into weeks. Meanwhile the General appeared to be doing nothing but talking with his savage visitors, stuffing them with wild turkey, venison and rum, exchanging gifts, and smoking the peace pipe.

Finally one morning General Wayne signaled for a bugle to be sounded. The notes had scarcely died away before he rose and addressed the Indians formally as they squatted, arms folded, before the council table. The result of his speech was the Treaty of Greenville, whereby the Indians agreed to give over to their "white brothers" two-thirds of the land that is now Ohio. In return, the Indians were paid on the spot $20,000 in goods—that is, in axes, muskets, hoes, gunpowder, blankets, and rum. They were also to receive $9,500 in goods for several years afterward. The Indians, in turn, had to surrender all the white prisoners they held.

After much wrangling and discussion among the chiefs, and a demand for ten more kegs of rum, the Indians agreed to accept the terms. Ninety-two chiefs and twenty-seven American officers, including Lieutenant Harrison, signed the treaty on August 3, 1795. After another feast, and pledges of peace back and forth, the Indians piled into their war canoes and went back to their villages. Both sides appeared pleased by the terms of the treaty.

It was Tecumseh alone who protested when he heard of the treaty. Over the years he had come to believe more and more that his people needed constant protection from the Long Knives and their shrewd business deals. He was as sincere now as he had been in his youth, in believing that the white settlers should be held back. Only now, as a man, he was more passionate and eloquent in his role of Indian protector. He vowed the time would come when the Treaty of Greenville would have no more effect than words written on water. He called his tribe to a war dance, and made plans to move his hunting grounds farther west.

With the peace treaty executed, General Wayne left a small detachment of troops at Fort Greenville and moved back to Fort Washington for the winter, taking Lieutenant Harrison and his other aides-de-camp with him.

Lieutenant Harrison was delighted by this move. Back at Fort Washington he lost no time in galloping over to North Bend to look for Anna Symmes. She received him with enough enthusiasm to make him return again and again. On about his sixth visit, however, Anna met him tearfully.

"Billy, Father doesn't want me to see you any more," Anna said, sobbing in his arms.

Lieutenant Harrison was both astounded and angry. "Why in heaven's name not?" he demanded.

"Father thinks soldiers—with possibly the exception of generals—are all scalawags, vagabonds, and adventurers," Anna said. "He just doesn't understand."

Lieutenant Harrison's face darkened. Why should Judge Symmes think so unkindly of soldiers, the very

"Anna," he said firmly, "we must elope!"

soldiers who were protecting his beautiful new home and his thousands of acres of land?

"Pray, let me see your father, Anna," he said. "I'll speak to him about us."

Anna shook her head. "No," she said, "it's hopeless, Billy. Anyway, Father's gone away for several weeks."

Several weeks! To Lieutenant Harrison this seemed like several years! Anna and he were both in love. They were of an age to make up their own minds. Why should they wait several weeks? He took her face in his hands and tilted her chin gently until he met her eyes. "Anna," he said firmly, "we must elope!"

At first, Anna Symmes was horrified by the idea of marrying without her father's consent. But after a time she realized that the choice lay between elopement and losing Billy Harrison. So she agreed to elope. A few days later the young couple slipped away and were married by a justice of the peace. Immediately they set up housekeeping in a log cabin just outside the Fort.

When Judge Symmes returned he raged and swore and roared a great deal privately about "horsewhipping this young whippersnapper who has somehow hypnotized my daughter!"

But inquiries he made around the Fort during the next two weeks convinced him that the young man who had won his daughter's heart was not such a bad catch after all. By the time he met his son-in-law for the first time at a farewell dinner for General Wayne, the Judge had calmed down considerably. Nevertheless, when the two found themselves alone after dinner, the Judge drew himself up and demanded, "And just how do you propose to support my daughter, young man?"

Lieutenant Harrison looked him straight in the eye, though his face paled. The two men glared at each other a moment without speaking. Then Lieutenant Harrison answered quietly, "My sword is my means of support, sir."

"Humph!" Judge Symmes snorted, though he was secretly impressed by the young man's dignity and his straightforward answer. "Humph! On army pay?" And he walked away.

It is said that two days later Judge Symmes invited Lieutenant Harrison to dinner at his new house in North Bend. By the time the two men said good-bye that evening, they were on the way to becoming friends.

11 · The Young Commander

It seemed almost as if gaining his father-in-law's blessing was a happy omen for the young Lieutenant. A few days after that, when General Wayne left for the East, he placed Fort Washington under Harrison's command. Further, he wrote the government recommending that the young commander be promoted to a captaincy.

Lieutenant Harrison could hardly believe his good luck. Anna was particularly pleased, because now her father would surely be impressed with her husband.

Although the promotion to captain did not come through until two years later, in 1797, Lieutenant Harrison and his young wife began to be treated with great respect throughout the community. All the problems of the district, both military and civil, came to their doorstep.

The town of Cincinnati, growing before their eyes, introduced the young couple to every kind of human situation. New settlers poured down the Ohio to stake out land claims. Between settling their disputes and keeping the long line of western forts in order, Lieutenant Harrison was kept busy day and night. He scarcely had time to be alone with his bride. Even after he had finished the day's work, he had to dispatch long reports to the army headquarters in Philadelphia, keeping them informed of activities on the frontier.

Lieutenant Harrison labored into the night over these written reports. At Hampden-Sidney College he had always been interested in reading, and had developed a sound knowledge of the principal Latin authors, but writing essays and compositions had not come easily to him.

Now he *had* to learn to write, clearly and lucidly. His

reports would be read by educated men who would judge him by what he said and how he said it. From his father-in-law's library he borrowed book after book in an effort to improve his vocabulary and sense of composition.

It was in Caesar's *Commentaries* that Lieutenant Harrison first found a style that appealed to him. The book presented rapidly and vividly, but with great simplicity, the events of history. Then in the *Odes* of Horace he came upon another model of good writing. It contained both common sense and high imagination. Finally he poured over Cicero's *Letters*. Studying this book, he saw that Cicero varied his writing style to fit his subject. His official letters were grave, controlled, and to the point. The letters wherein he was trying to persuade someone to a new opinion were more passionate and eloquent. His private letters remained intimate and easy, filled with racy everyday speech and observations.

Fortunately, Anna Harrison understood completely why her husband studied and scribbled far into the night. She knew he was quietly ambitious, and that his new position of authority made him take his work seriously. But, more importantly, she realized that he represented the government on the frontier. The government back in Philadelphia depended on his reports, his "eyes", to tell them what was happening. The reports needed to be well presented, no matter how much work it cost him.

Yet Anna was half relieved when, the following year, a letter came from the government suggesting that her husband resign from the army and accept the political appointment of Secretary of the Northwest Territory.

Lieutenant Harrison faced his wife with the letter. "What shall I do?" he asked. "I'm a soldier, Anna, and now they want me to be a politician."

"It's a great honor, Billy," Anna said quietly. "You're only twenty-five and already you are offered a fine opportunity to serve your country. Think how important this new land out here is." And then she added, "Also, we could have a real home, and maybe you won't have to be away fighting Indians."

That night Lieutenant Harrison wrote out his acceptance and sent it East on the first passing riverboat.

12 · *The Young Administrator*

For the next two years, William Henry Harrison studied the land laws of the Northwest Territory and tried to learn how to handle the varied claims and disputes that daily streamed over his desk. He was pleased to find himself gaining confidence with each passing month, and pleased, too, that the older settlers no longer seemed shocked to find so young a man sitting in judgment on their affairs.

When the Territory acquired sufficient population by 1799 to be given a delegate in Congress, William Henry was selected, for by this time no one else knew as much as he about the needs of the new land.

Arriving in Philadelphia, William Henry found that a great many important things had happened in the previous eight years about which he knew very little. Eli Whitney's cotton gin, patented in 1792, had been stepping up the production of cotton all through the South. Everyone said the cotton gin would soon revolutionize industry in America, change slavery, and make the South prosperous. And a man named Charles Newbold had introduced an *iron* plow, which farmers everywhere were beginning to use to advantage.

There was, of course, a new President also. Washington had made his famous "Farewell Address" to public life in 1796 and gone back to his fine farm at Mount Vernon, Virginia. John Adams of Massachusetts was now President, and Thomas Jefferson was Vice-President. They had been in office since March 4, 1797.

Further, three new states had been added to the orig-

William Henry Harrison in 1800.

inal thirteen: the Green Mountain State of Vermont in 1791; Kentucky, popularly known as the Blue Grass State, had come in a year later; and in 1796 the Volunteer State of Tennessee had followed. Obviously the country was growing fast. Affairs in Congress were certain to be many and lively. Would anyone listen to the new delegate from the West?

At his first opportunity to speak, young William Henry Harrison laid before Congress what he considered to be the most critical problem of the Northwest Territory: a change in the law that would allow settlers to buy small farms. Carried away by his subject, he spoke for two hours. He had begun fearfully, but after a while he almost forgot his audience. When he finished, there was little applause. In fact, some of the members had risen and left the small circular chamber even while he was speaking. He thought, too, that from time to time he had caught several yawns on the faces of members who stayed to hear him through.

He returned to his wife that evening feeling very discouraged. "I spoke too long, Anna. And not very well, I reckon. I fear I failed."

It was true that not every Congressman had been impressed by the new delegate or his subject. For one thing, the Northwest Territory seemed very far away. Its problems were not their problems, the Congress felt. Then, too, while young Harrison spoke well enough, and seemed to be educated enough to quote Latin, he was rather long-winded, and maybe a little too earnest for a newcomer. He hadn't included a single joke in his entire speech.

But the next day Harrison found a message on his desk from Vice-President Jefferson. Jefferson had been greatly taken by the speech and wanted to confer with him.

The result of this meeting was that Harrison introduced an important bill in Congress. It was called a "land bill," and although it contained many "whys" and "wherefores" and compromises before it was passed by the lawmakers, it had in it the important passages Harrison had set forth in his speech.

What Harrison wanted for the Territory was a greater opportunity for more settlers to buy land and make homes. Under the Land Act of 1796, approximately half the lands of the Territory were to be disposed of in tracts containing 5,770 acres. The remainder were to be sold in tracts of 640 acres, with a minimum price of $2 an acre.

Harrison stood before the members of Congress and spoke with youthful earnestness and directness about the situation. He explained that the Land Act then in existence was favorable only to wealthy speculators and real-estate companies who could afford to buy such large pieces of land. Obviously the average settler could not buy land in such quantity. Harrison asked the Congress to pass a law allowing land to be sold in the Territory in plots of 320 acres, so that men with small capital could come to the new country, buy land, and settle.

He said a lot more on the subject of the opportunities afforded to the country if the new land were properly settled. The Congress listened, but did not act immediately. Days passed. Finally, with Thomas Jefferson's support, and after Harrison had patiently visited the leading Congressmen to explain the importance of the law he was presenting, the bill passed, after some minor additions by the Senate. It was a great day for the United States when this happened. Few people realized it at that time, but it was Harrison's land bill that did as much as anything to encourage ordinary people to flock to the new country so that new states could be formed.

In 1800 the Northwest Territory was divided. The greater portion of it was named Indiana and its capital was established at Vincennes, the growing settlement on the Wabash River. (When the southeast part of the Territory had the required 60,000 inhabitants it became the new state of Ohio, in 1803.)

Harrison, though only twenty-seven years old, was appointed Governor of the Indiana Territory. Congress instructed him to proceed to the West and take up residence. This he was glad to do, for he loved that part of the country.

Accompanied by his wife, Harrison arrived in Vincennes in 1801. With one secretary and three judges, he was now the administrator of this whole vast land where only ten years before he had come as a shy young lieutenant. The appointment, he knew, was a great honor, but it meant there was a tremendous task to be done, too. Harrison went at it slowly, methodically, tirelessly. In the next few years he made many friends and some enemies, as people in power usually do, but he kept his job as Governor.

By 1803 he was eager and ready to build the home

that Anna had long wanted. In a walnut grove outside Vincennes he erected a large, comfortable brick dwelling which he named "Grouseland" because of the many birds in the region. One room became his office, and the spacious tree-shaded lawn was laid out as a meeting place for political conferences with the settlers, and powwows with the Indians.

Harrison entertained generously at "Grouseland." In one year he served three hundred and sixty-five hams to his guests, and eight hundred barrels of apple cider.

13 · *The Young Governor*

From 1801 to 1811, Governor Harrison was totally absorbed in his new duties. These were so numerous that the powers granted him by the government were almost those of a king.

Here is what he had to do: He had to adopt such laws, criminal and civil, as might be necessary and suitable to the conditions of a new country. He appointed all judges, and all civil and military officers below the rank of general. He commanded the militia. Beyond this, it was his job to divide the more populated areas into counties and townships. He dealt with Indian affairs and, as sole commissioner, met with the Indians to make treaties and erect land boundaries between the Ohio River, the Great Lakes, and the Mississippi. So he was very busy, with scarcely any time left to go hunting and fishing, which he particularly liked to do.

His greatest administrative problem was lack of ready communication. The white population was thinly scattered over a wide area. When Harrison became Governor there were only two other principal settlements in the whole Territory besides Vincennes. One was known as Clark's Grant, at the falls of the Ohio. The other, called the American Bottom, was an area stretching from Kaskaskia to Cahokia, in what is now Illinois.

The land between settlements was still occupied by Indians, with only an occasional lonely pioneer cabin. Although it was a period of professed peace with the Indians, they were always in a state of irritation. They were still spurred on by British trappers and agents who supplied them readily with rum and arms and a steady suspicion and hatred of the Americans.

Nevertheless, in the course of his administration as

Governor, Harrison concluded thirteen important treaties with the different tribes. He obtained land grants for the United States of not less than 60,000,000 acres.

Of course he had not done all this easily. He had done it only by hard work and by holding to a consistent policy of firmness combined with moderation and integrity. To both Indian and white, his word was known throughout the Territory to be as good as his written promise.

In 1805, when there were enough people in the Territory to justify voting and a regular elected government, Governor Harrison offered to resign. He thought his work was done. But Thomas Jefferson, now the third President of the United States, persuaded him to continue in office.

President Jefferson knew how important it was to have a courageous man of skill and leadership in pioneer country. Jefferson had a real vision of the possible expansion of the United States. In 1803 he had purchased Louisiana from France, acquiring land which doubled the size of the country. This new land extended from the Mississippi to the Rocky Mountains, with the island where New Orleans now stands thrown in for good measure. Also, in 1804 Jefferson had sent Meriwether Lewis and William Clark, early army friends of Harrison's, across America to explore the country as far as the Pacific Ocean. Small wonder that Jefferson wanted a man who understood the importance of pioneer country to stay on as governor.

The people of the Indiana Territory soon showed that they liked Harrison as much as Jefferson did. In fact, they sent a unanimous resolution about their fine governor to Washington, D.C., where the new national government had been moved from Philadelphia.

The resolution said: "We (the House of Representatives of the Indiana Territory) urge the reappointment of our present Governor, William Henry Harrison:—because he possesses the good wishes and affections of a great majority of his fellow-citizens; because we believe him to be sincerely attached to the Union, the prosperity of the United States, and the administration of its government, and because we have confidence in his virtues, talents, and republicanism."

When Governor Harrison read a copy of the letter at his desk in "Grouseland," he was pleased but a little doubtful.

"I may end up with an arrow in my chest," he is reported to have said to his wife, "unless we learn to get along better with the Indians."

Without commenting further, he turned back to his work, to the endless reports he found necessary to write to the government, and which he got out painstakingly and dutifully, as the records show, during his entire public career.

14 · Chief Tecumseh's Warning

As the years passed, Governor Harrison continued his efforts to acquire more land for white settlers.

At the Treaty of Fort Wayne in 1809, he had sat down with the chiefs of the Miami, Potawatami, and Delaware tribes to buy a large tract of land in western Indiana. Tecumseh of the Shawnees did not come to this meeting, but when he heard the land had been sold, he was furious. Tecumseh said that no Indian tribe had the right to sell land unless all the other tribes agreed. He threatened both Harrison and the chiefs who had made the Treaty with violence. He said the Treaty was illegal.

Hearing how disturbed the Shawnees were, and fearing bloodshed, Governor Harrison wrote them a letter addressed to the Shawnee headquarters on the Tippecanoe River. The Shawnees had moved there two years before and founded a village where the Tippecanoe and Wabash rivers meet, near what is now Lafayette, Indiana. The town soon became known as the Prophet's Town.

A man named Joseph Barron was chosen by Harrison to deliver the letter. But when Barron got to the Shawnee village, Tecumseh was not there. Barron was received by the haughty Prophet himself, who made the messenger stand at a distance of twelve feet while he read the letter.

When the Prophet finished reading the letter he looked at the messenger contemptuously. "You are a spy!" he shouted. "There is your grave. Look at it!" He pointed to the ground where Barron stood. Barron trembled and looked around for a chance to escape.

At this moment Tecumseh entered. When he saw what was happening he rebuked his brother, the Prophet, for his threat to the messenger. Then he picked up the letter from Governor Harrison, called for his half-breed interpreter, and had the letter read to him.

Governor Harrison's communication was to the point. It said, "Brothers, and warriors of the great tribe of Shaw-nee: What reason have you to complain of the United States? Have they taken anything from you? Have they ever violated the treaties made with the red men? You say they have purchased land from those who had no right to sell. Show the truth of this and the land will be instantly restored. Show us the rightful owners. Let them present themselves. The ears of your Father in Washington will be open to their complaints. If you would carry your complaints before your great Father, the President, you may do so. I will take the means to send you, and three chiefs to be chosen by you, to the city where your Father lives. Everything necessary shall be prepared for your journey, and means taken to insure your safe return."

When the interpreter finished, Tecumseh's face was stern.

"Return to your Father, the Governor," he said to the messenger. "Tell him I shall visit him within a short time. I shall reply to his message in person."

Barron hurried away, glad to be out of sight of the scowling faces of the Shawnees and their chief.

When Governor Harrison heard that Tecumseh wished to pay him a visit, he feared some treachery. He sent Barron back with the request that Tecumseh come to him with only a few warriors, and come unarmed. Tecumseh, this time, sent the messenger away without any reply.

Two weeks later Tecumseh and seventy-five painted and fully armed warriors appeared at the Governor's house at Vincennes. The Governor was secretly alarmed when they approached, but he tried to show no fear. He did, however, immediately call for his armed guard of twelve men. With muskets loaded and side-arms ready, they came and stood behind the Governor's high-backed council chair, which had been placed on the lawn at "Grouseland."

This was the first formal meeting of Harrison and Tecumseh since the Treaty of Greenville. While they waited, looking at each other, the Governor was quick to note that Tecumseh had not changed. His features were still noble, his eyes intelligent, his whole bearing poised and dignified. He wore little jewelry, only a single brass bracelet and a handsome locket of quartz. His face was unpainted, his body unmarked. He did not look like a savage.

"Truly, an impressive Indian," Governor Harrison commented later in one of his letters. "I knew I would have to deal with him cautiously."

And Tecumseh, estimating the lean, grave features of the Governor, and the penetrating blue eyes that met his unwaveringly, felt equally sure that he was dealing with a man who would not be easily put down.

So they faced each other across the lawn at "Grouseland," while the hot August sun glared down on them. Governor Harrison seated himself in the shade of a sturdy walnut tree and invited Tecumseh to take the chair opposite him. Tecumseh politely refused, then squatted on the bare ground.

"I prefer to place myself on the bosom of my Mother, the earth," he said through his interpreter.

The formal council began with Tecumseh delivering a long speech.

Tecumseh paid Governor Harrison a visit at "Grouseland."

"Brother," Tecumseh said, "I wish you to listen to me well. I wish to reply to you explicitly, as I think you do not clearly understand what I said to you before. I shall explain it again." Tecumseh went on to say that first the French had come into Indian lands and asked to be the "Father" of the Indians. Then the British had come and asked the same thing. And now the Americans were doing it. Tecumseh explained that the Indians did not want any "white Father," for the "white Father" had excited jealousies between the tribes and taken their land.

"The Great Spirit," Tecumseh insisted, "said He gave this great island to His red children. He placed the whites on the other side of the big water. They were not contented with their own land, but came to take ours from us. They have driven us from the sea to the lakes. We can go no farther. They have taken it upon themselves to say this tract belongs to the Miamis, this to the Delawares and so on, but the Great Spirit intended it as the common property of all the tribes. Nor can it be sold without the consent of all. Our 'Father' tells us that we have no business on the Wabash, that the land belongs to other tribes. But the Great Spirit ordered us to come here and here we shall stay."

He folded his arms and waited for the interpreter, keeping his eyes boldly fixed on Governor Harrison.

After a few moments Tecumseh went on to say that in "two moons we shall assemble"—he nodded toward the other chiefs—"at the Huron village to declare that if we sell land to the white man, all tribes must join in the sale. The Red Men are all of one great nation."

Governor Harrison answered quietly, but with great firmness. "Brother, you have spoken well," he replied. "But many of your words are mistaken. In the first place, the Red Men are not all brothers of one nation. If it were the intention of the Great Spirit to make you all brothers, why has He put six different tongues in your heads? Why do you not all speak one language? Such land as we have bought from other tribes we have paid for. These other tribes are satisfied. Why must the Shawnee tribe object? Does the Shawnee tribe own all the lands between the seas?"

Tecumseh's face darkened as the interpreter repeated the Governor's words.

"Has not our Great Father in Washington treated you fairly?" Governor Harrison asked. "Has he not treated all the Red Men fairly? True, bad men among you and bad men among us have raised the tomahawk and gun against one another. But we have kept faith with you in our treaties. We have pledged our word to buy your lands and not to seize them from you without payment."

Governor Harrison was interrupted at this point by Tecumseh, who sprang to his feet and with angry gestures poured out his denial of Harrison's words. As Tecumseh shouted, his warriors sprang to his side and raised their war clubs and tomahawks threateningly.

"What does he say?" Governor Harrison quickly asked the interpreter.

"Tecumseh says you lie—that the white men are all great liars and should go back across the sea where they were born," the interpreter explained.

Hearing this, Governor Harrison acted at once. He pulled his sword from its scabbard and advanced a step toward Tecumseh. "Say to the chief of the Shawnee that I will not listen to his insults. Say that if he continues I shall put out our council fire!"

For a tense moment it looked as if Tecumseh and his warriors would attack the handful of white men facing them. But something in the determined countenance of Governor Harrison and his men made Tecumseh hesitate.

After a long interval Tecumseh apologized to Governor Harrison for his heated words and the conference was resumed. But throughout the exchanges that followed Tecumseh said repeatedly, "I want the white man to go. I want our hunting lands restored. I want no more land sold to the Long Knives."

Governor Harrison listened patiently and tried again and again to explain that the treaties now in existence must remain. When Tecumseh finally saw that Governor Harrison would yield no ground he became angry again and signaled to his warriors and the visiting chiefs. They all turned and walked to their war canoes without a word.

At the bank of the river Tecumseh hurled back a parting threat. "If the Great White Father in Washington does not have sense enough to understand me, then there will be much trouble!"

Harrison replied in much the same spirit of firmness

that he had shown in earlier communications with the Shawnee tribe. "Brother," he said, "I am myself of the Long Knife Fire. As soon as they [the American soldiers] hear my voice you will see them pouring into battle their swarms of hunting-shirt men, as numerous as the mosquitoes on the shores of the Wabash."

Tecumseh listened but made no reply. With another signal he directed his party into their war canoes and, after a few moments, the Indians paddled away. Governor Harrison and his men sighed with uneasy relief as they stood watching the long, snakelike line of canoes disappear up the river.

15 · *Marching North*

"The difficult thing is," Governor Harrison admitted to his wife later that night, "I half agree with Tecumseh. It's true that white men have taken the Indians' lands. To be sure, we have paid for them. But not enough. And, as Tecumseh says, their lives were peaceful before we came to this continent." He sighed heavily, while he removed his clay-stained boots. "I suppose one must say that our people bring civilization, and that civilization can't be held back. Yet if I were an Indian, I would fight back."

These were the Governor's private thoughts, which he repeated many times to his friends. But his sense of realism proved, in the end, to be greater than his private sympathies with the Indians. He knew almost instinctively that he must prepare to fight Tecumseh. If he did not, many innocent white people would be scalped. Sooner or later, by the very weight of numbers, the white man would take over this country. It was better, he thought, to meet the situation immediately.

Tired as he was, he nevertheless took up his quill pen and wrote a letter to the War Department in Washington asking that a regiment be sent to Vincennes at once. He knew he must act promptly. Tecumseh would certainly lose no time in arousing the other tribes for battle, now that he had made a public threat to fight.

The next day Governor Harrison was up at dawn. "Post a bulletin asking for volunteers to the militia," he ordered. "Circulate it through the entire Territory, and as far south as Kentucky."

In a few weeks enough public-spirited men had responded to form the basis of a small army. Eight hundred men had volunteered out of Kentucky and Indiana, and four hundred regular soldiers came from the East. All that autumn, and through the spring of 1811, Governor Harrison drilled them.

When summer came, the Governor received orders from the government to take the rank of general, and to move northward up the Wabash River with the army toward Tecumseh's headquarters. His orders did not call for war. The government's intention was merely to let the Indians know that the white men were fully prepared. It was hoped that this show of strength would be enough to avoid bloodshed.

General Harrison devised the strategy for the marching army, and appointed all the ranks of command. On September 22, 1811, he addressed the thousand men who were to form the expedition. "The whole army will parade tomorrow at one o'clock; the infantry in two columns of single file. The regular troops will form the leading battalions of each column; the militia infantry, the rear."

The soldiers cheered, for this was the command for action. General Harrison raised his hand for silence, then went on with his orders. "Major Daveiss will place his largest troop of dragoons in a squadron at open order 150 yards in advance of the columns of infantry, and at right angles to the order of march. The next largest troop will be placed in the same form at 150 yards in the rear of the columns. The third troop will be placed, in single line, on the right flank, at 150 yards from the line of infantry, and parallel thereto. Captain Spencer's company will form and march on the left flank, in the same manner."

Both men and officers listened attentively, for by this time they were convinced that their commanding officer knew his job.

"The army, thus formed," Harrison continued, "will commence its march—the columns taking care to keep their distance and their heads dressed. When in the woods, the movements will be regulated by signals from the drums."

More specific written orders were then dispatched to each officer, and the historic march started. A surgeon and a surgeon's mate accompanied the men.

By October 3rd the American army had reached the east side of the Wabash River, two miles north of the present site of Terre Haute, Indiana. (Terre Haute, named by the French, means "high ground.") Here General Harrison sent forward two scouts to try to discover what the reaction of the Indians was to his advancing army.

The scouts returned with startling news. "Tecumseh is not in his village," the first scout reported. "He has gone south to arouse the tribes there against the whites."

General Harrison smiled. He had known for weeks that Tecumseh was away. That was why he had chosen this time to march.

"What about the Prophet?" the General inquired.

"He is holding great war dances every night. The friendly Delawares all say he will fight. He wants to gain prestige by winning a battle against us before his brother Tecumseh returns," the scout explained. "The Prophet boasts that he will burn alive the first white prisoner taken."

General Harrison nodded, then called his men together to let them know about the Prophet's boast. He felt the men would fight harder and not allow themselves to be taken prisoners if they knew of the fate hanging over them.

To gain time, and because he still hoped to avoid open

conflict, General Harrison ordered a fort to be built at Terre Haute. Perhaps a fort so near their town would still scare off the Indians. The fort was completed in three weeks, and by unanimous request of the officers and men it was named Fort Harrison.

Just as the fort was finished, however, the Prophet rashly sent some of his tribe sneaking down to steal some American cavalry horses. The raid was made during the night and the Indians got away with ten horses. When General Harrison learned of this thievery he was indignant. He dispatched a stern note demanding that the stolen horses be returned. The note was ignored by the Prophet.

On the following day, the army resumed its march toward the Prophet's Town. Each company now proceeded with great caution. Two routes, one on each side of the Wabash River, led to the Indian camp. The route on the left side was shorter and General Harrison's officers suggested it as the one to follow.

But General Harrison, who knew the Indians well, shook his head. "It's shorter, yes—but it goes through wooded country. It would expose us to ambush. After

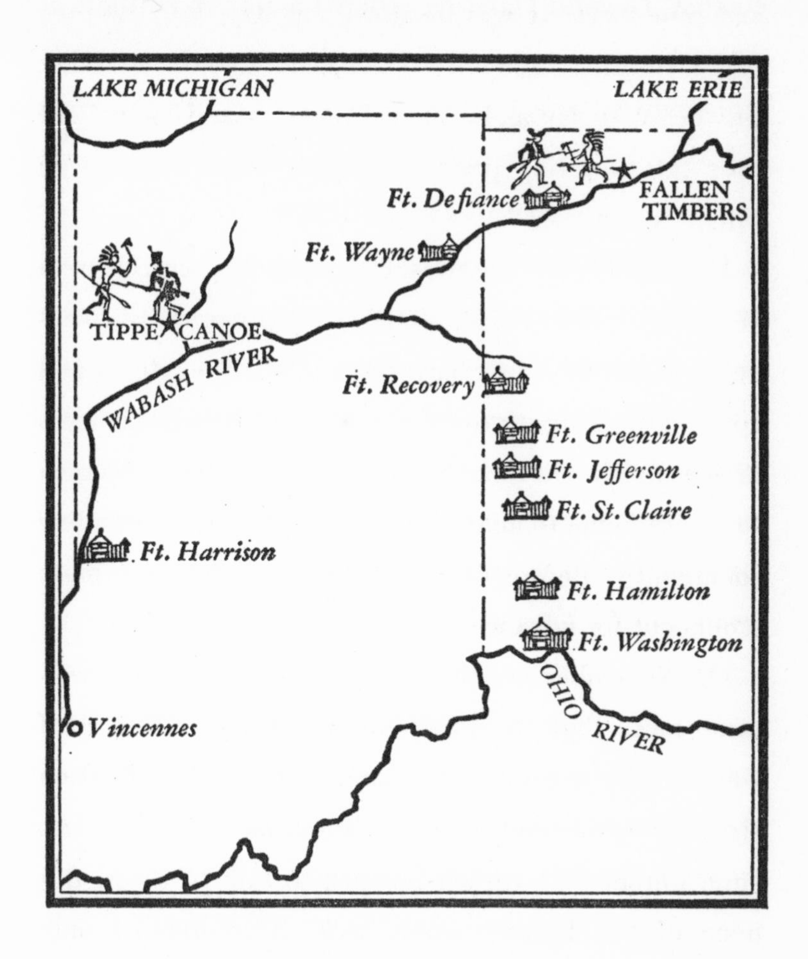

we cross Raccoon Creek, we shall take the right-side trail."

The next few days they marched close to the river. Above them were high, rocky bluffs covered by cedar and pine trees. It was beautiful country, but the men had little time to admire it. One old soldier, however, was heard to say as he shaded his eyes and looked out over the flowering prairie, "Country like this is sure worth fightin' for!"

Up till this time, the advancing army had scarcely seen an Indian. General Harrison began to worry. He wondered if possibly the Shawnees had left their town and gone on the warpath to raid isolated pioneer settlements farther north. He thought of detaching some of his men to return home to guard Vincennes and the surrounding community. Before doing so, however, he sent more scouts out for advance information.

On November 5th the scouts returned with the welcome news that the Prophet's Town was still full of warriors. By evening of the same day General Harrison sighted several Indians lurking about on the trail ahead. Interpreters were rushed forward to talk to them. But none of the Indians would talk. They replied only with scowls and defiant gestures. They were all in full warpaint.

On the afternoon of the following day, the army had moved within a mile and a half of the Prophet's Town.

The soldiers now became tense and excited and urged General Harrison to attack at once. But General Harrison refused. He patiently explained that his military orders were to avoid hostilities if possible. Forthwith, he ordered Captain Dubois and an interpreter to display a flag of truce and to go forward to the Indian camp and ask for a peace conference with the Prophet.

But the Indians refused to talk to Captain Dubois. General Harrison determined, then, to march even nearer to the town and encamp for the night. As his army started to move again, three Indians and a chief counselor suddenly appeared and asked to speak with "their Great Father, the Governor." General Harrison invited them to his tent.

The Indian deputation, with much pretended innocence, inquired at once why the American army had marched so near to their town. They insisted that the Prophet and all the Shawnees felt most friendly toward the white men. They even said the Prophet himself wished on the following day to talk with General Harrison and conclude a treaty of peace.

General Harrison listened patiently. When the Indians rose to go, he sent his "greetings" to the Prophet and said he looked forward to a peaceful discussion on the morrow. Then he inquired of the Indians for a suitable camping ground for his army. He wanted them to know that he was prepared to keep his troops near by as long as necessary.

The Indians immediately suggested a camping site northwest of their town where the shallow Tippecanoe River meets the Wabash. General Harrison thanked them and dispatched two officers to inspect the suggested ground.

When the officers came back, they reported that the place offered plenty of fuel and water and looked satisfactory. So the necessary orders were given and the army moved up and went into camp for the night.

16 · *Battle of Tippecanoe*

Yet when General Harrison himself inspected the camping site the Indians had chosen for his army, he was not pleased. It was pleasant enough ground for camping—a high spot with good oak land, well above the marshy prairie, and a fresh-running creek at the bottom. But the river was densely skirted on both sides by willow shrubs. With this protection, it would be very easy for the Indians to sneak up during the night and surprise the army.

The General thought first of ordering the army to find a new spot, then decided to stay, as the men were exhausted from their march. To be prepared for the danger of a night attack, however, he doubled the number of sentries and ordered the men to sleep with their guns loaded and ready for battle. He also placed his best company of mounted riflemen, known as the Yellow-jackets because of their uniforms, in a forward position on the vulnerable right flank. The dragoons were told to parade dismounted, with pistols in their belts, as a reserve corps. The campfires were ordered banked so that the firelight would not reveal the position of the sleeping soldiers. With these precautions taken, General Harrison lay down with his clothes on in the hope of getting a few hours of sleep.

At four o'clock the next morning, the General got to his feet to inspect his army. The sun was not yet up when he pushed back his tent flap and stepped outside. He looked toward the creek where the ghostly night mist was rising. Suddenly, on the left, he heard a shot fired by the sentinel. The next thing he heard were the savage war whoops of the Shawnees. In the semi-darkness, the shouts seemed very close.

General Harrison ran right and left, giving the alarm and shouting his orders. "To arms! To arms! Take your posts!"

The drowsy soldiers, fumbling for their weapons, barely had time to get to their feet before the first arrows and bullets whizzed by them. A few bold Shawnees even penetrated into the encampment before their wild yells were silenced by sword thrusts and answering gunfire.

For at least an hour the whole scene was one of horror and confusion. It was still dark, and the only light came from the uncertain flicker of the banked campfires. The American soldiers had much trouble finding their companies, and more trouble finding the enemy, who from their secure positions outside could see where to pour their fire.

General Harrison, mounted on his horse now, raced through the camp shouting his many orders. "Put the fires out! Close the right flank! Reinforce the left. Close ranks."

Suddenly a bullet went through the General's hat and knocked it off. Another bullet grazed his skull and sent the blood trickling down his face. He seemed not to notice, for he went on calling out his orders, encouraging the men, instructing them how to keep their lines intact. His hope was to keep the enemy from breaking through the outposts before daylight. If the lines could hold until then, he would order a cavalry charge, then a bayonet charge. He knew from other battles that the Indians hated and feared the bayonet beyond all other forms of attack.

When the first murky light filtered down from the cloudy sky, General Harrison surveyed the scene before him. He was not encouraged by what he saw. The ground was thick with fallen soldiers. The groans of the wounded and dying came up to him as he galloped from right to left flank urging his men on. Yet the sight of the exposed, hatless General riding back and forth in the teeth of the enemy's fire cheered the men beyond measure. They gave him a quick "hurrah" as he passed, primed their guns, and fought on.

The daylight soon revealed many of the enemy clustered in the trees, firing their arrows through open gaps in the foliage, then protecting themselves by hugging the tree trunks as they fitted more arrows into their bows. But as the American gunfire steadied, and the confused

He galloped from right to left flank urging his men on.

soldiers sighted the enemy, the painted warriors began to drop and tumble from the trees like leaves.

Yet the fight did not slacken. The Indians fought on with great daring and courage. Some of them seemed almost to ask for death. They charged forward straight into the American guns, or swung down from the trees flourishing their tomahawks and shouting defiance, even at the very moment they were being struck down.

General Harrison sighted the Prophet himself on a ridge near by. The ridge was at a safe distance from the scene of battle, and from this comfortable spot the Prophet shouted constant encouragement to his followers, exhorting them to sacrifice themselves, predicting defeat for the whites, and promising his race a sure and glorious victory.

Behind the Prophet the squaws and children stood in small knots, watching the battle's progress. From time to time they shrieked and wailed with the Prophet, their chanting voices rising shrill and thin above the hoarse cries of the warriors and the wild neighing of the horses.

The battle raged for three long hours. Only in the last thirty minutes was it clear which side would win. General Harrison had already ordered three bayonet charges. But each time the men plunged forward they were driven back.

On the fourth charge, General Harrison himself rode out in front, waved his men to follow, and commanded them to advance at all costs. Up and down the line the rolling drums beat out the signal to attack. The flag-bearers raised their banners high. The officers shouted and brandished their sabers. Running half-crouched, the men advanced, their long muskets with their shafts of steel searching the enemy.

The Indians met the last charge head-on. For fifteen minutes the whole field was a mass of grappling bodies. Sword met tomahawk, musket met battle-ax in a wild hand-to-hand encounter. The Prophet, seeing his warriors fall, became seized with a frenzy. His war chants increased in volume, and his body writhed in a grotesque and mad dance, as if he were possessed of a thousand devils.

Finally, the Prophet gave one long piercing wail, louder than all the rest. At once the Indians who were still able to fight fell back. They picked up their dead, then suddenly took to their heels and ran. At that, the tired soldiers shouted and poured a last round of shot into their scattering flight.

The battle of Tippecanoe was over. General Harrison and his brave men had broken the last great Indian army to be assembled east of the Mississippi. Thirty-seven Americans had been killed, including nine officers, and one hundred and seventy-nine had been wounded. The Indian losses were thought to be even heavier, though it was impossible to get an accurate account, because the Indians, as always, had carried away as many fallen warriors as they could.

General Harrison ordered that the dead Americans be buried in a mass grave, each with a flag wrapped around his body. Logs were then burned over the grave in an attempt to conceal the spot from animals and marauding Indians. Prayers were said, and a salute was fired over the burial place. The bugle sounded over the rolling hills as a last tribute to the fallen heroes.

17 · *Last Wars with the Indians*

The day after the great battle the American army moved into the Prophet's Town. It was found to be deserted, except for one forlorn old chief who had stayed behind because of a broken leg. The American army surgeon set the leg, and then General Harrison came up to speak with the chief.

The General was greatly surprised by what the old

chief told him. He learned, for the first time, that the American army had been fighting not just the Shawnees, but warriors from many other tribes as well: the Hurons, Kickapoos, Potawatamies, Winnebagoes, Ottawas, Chippewas, Sacs, and Miamis. Also, three great Indian chiefs had been in the battle: White-Loon, Winnemac, and Stone-Eater. So, actually, part of the union of Indians Tecumseh had dreamed about had been involved in the fighting. With the defeat of all these tribes in one engagement, Tecumseh's great confederacy had been seriously damaged, if not broken.

Hearing this, General Harrison felt better about the losses his army had suffered. Yet he still wondered what Tecumseh would do when he returned from the South and found his people scattered. Would he rally them for another battle?

To make sure, at least, that the Prophet's Town would never again be an Indian rallying point, General Harrison reluctantly ordered that the village and everything in it be burned. This was done, though the ragged and hungry army saved large quantities of corn and dried deer meat, and some brass kettles for souvenirs, before they scattered their flaming torches through the village.

Then the army turned away from the blazing town and marched back to Fort Harrison. The wounded, hauled in wagons, accompanied them.

At Fort Harrison the General sat down, amid the cheers of the welcoming settlers, to get off a dispatch to the War Department in Washington about the battle. In his dispatch he praised the courage and valor of his officers and men. He also added his hope that "their glorious stand at the Battle of Tippecanoe would end, for all time, the Indian trouble in the Indiana Territory."

But the General had no more than returned to Vincennes when he heard that the British agents were again stirring up the savages farther north in a last hope of retaining some part of the Indiana Territory for themselves. Also, Tecumseh had returned and, hearing of his tribe's defeat, had joined with the British.

New orders soon came West from the War Department asking that General Harrison assume the position of commander-in-chief of the United States Army of the

Northwest. His instructions were to prepare a new army in case the British struck.

A few months later, the British army openly attacked American forts around Detroit and Lake Erie. After these attacks, the War of 1812 officially began, and once more General Harrison was in the field.

To relieve Fort Wayne, which was under siege, General Harrison ordered men and supplies to be assembled at Lake Erie. Another unit was dispatched to Fort Meigs. By April, 1813, this fort was also under siege. After twelve days of intense fighting, General Harrison held the fort and drove off the British commander, Proctor.

Then General Harrison marshaled his men and marched on, quartering his army at Sandusky Bay. Here he waited for further orders. But the delay made some of his soldiers restive and homesick, particularly the militiamen from Kentucky. Word came to the General that many men planned to desert, or to mutiny against their officers. General Harrison immediately sounded an "alarm" and, with drums, called the troops before him at four o'clock in the morning. He directed that the men form in a hollow square around him. Then he mounted his charger and addressed them.

As always, his manner was courteous and solemn, but now his face plainly showed the grief he felt over the planned mutiny. In the beginning of his speech the General expressed regret that "dissatisfaction and discontent have appeared in my ranks, and especially among those I have been accustomed to regard as devoted and self-denying patriots." He looked out over the listening men, searching for clues to their feelings and temper.

When he continued, his voice was still sad, his words gentle and reasonable. "It is true," he said, "the war and its hardships are before you. The quiets and comforts of home are not to be found in the fields and forests, in the storms and contests through which you must wander, and which you must all experience as soldiers. If, then, any of you are disheartened, you are at liberty to retire." Again he waited. There were whispers among the men, but no one left the field.

Turning to the regiment in which the spirit of mutiny had first appeared, he raised his voice for the first time.

"Brave Kentuckians," he said, "is it you who are faint-hearted? You, in whose veins flow blood drawn from sires who never cowered in the field of battle? How will those sires receive you? Will you fill your wives and daughters with shame?" He looked straight into their upturned eyes.

Suddenly Colonel Scott, the senior Kentucky officer, shouted, "Come, fellow-soldiers, give the hero of Tippecanoe three cheers in token of your satisfaction, your patriotism, and your determination to abide by the cause for which we came here."

The soldiers broke into long cheers. The mutiny was over.

A few days later General Harrison learned that Admiral Oliver Hazard Perry, with the American Navy, had won a victory on Lake Erie. This was the General's signal to move. He crossed the lake quickly to attack the Redcoat Proctor who, with Tecumseh, had re-grouped his army in Canada. The combined British and Indian forces fled at General Harrison's approach, but were overtaken at the river Thames. Here, on October 15, 1813, General Harrison and the American army won another decisive victory. The British troops were surrounded, and Tecumseh was killed in the fiercely contested battle. Tecumseh died gallantly, as he had lived, fighting for what he believed. Most historians now recognize that this Shawnee chieftain was one of the noblest representatives of his race.

In other parts of the country the war raged on. The Americans won another naval battle at Plattsburg on Lake Champlain. In the south and southwest General Andrew Jackson broke the military power of the Creek Indians who were helping the British, and then proceeded to New Orleans where he successfully defended that great port from British guns.

On the eastern seaboard the British forces attacked and burned the capital city of Washington, but were finally thrown back at Baltimore with heavy losses.

After all these defeats, both the Indians and the British were ready for peace. The Treaty of Ghent in 1814 secured for the United States the boundaries that now divide our country from Canada.

Tecumseh died gallantly, as he had lived.

18 · The Passing Years

At last General Harrison thought he could return to his home and enjoy a peaceful life on his new farm at North Bend, Ohio. But again there were public demands on his time. In 1816, grateful citizens elected him to fill a vacancy in the House of Representatives. He served for two years, declining to be a candidate again in 1818.

But almost immediately he was chosen to be a member of the Ohio State Senate. Here he served another two years. When this public work was behind him, he headed once more toward his farm, hopeful of staying there forever.

Yet the voters of Ohio had different plans for their hero. In 1824 they elected him to public office once more, this time as United States Senator. Four more years were spent in Washington, D.C. When this long term of office was drawing to a close, President Adams asked General Harrison to accept the appointment of United States Minister to Colombia, in South America. He accepted, more out of financial need than feelings of patriotism, and stayed there until the new President, Andrew Jackson, called him back a year later.

Very little is recorded of General Harrison's life in Colombia. Yet it is known that in his brief time there he gave great encouragement and aid to Simón Bolívar, the famous democratic leader of the country. He also brought back one startling memento of his journey. It was a bright-feathered macaw, one of the most beautiful birds of South America.

Back in North Bend, Ohio, the General devoted the next ten years to running his 3,000-acre farm. He was happy on the farm. Behind him were many public honors, and he had given freely of his energies to the country's service. Now he was content to lead a quiet life, to be a bystander, for he believed that his country no longer needed him.

A great many things had been happening to the United States and to the Northwest Territory. The state of Indiana had been carved out of the Territory and admitted to statehood in 1816. Illinois had followed in 1818. All of Florida had been ceded from Spain. The important Monroe Doctrine had been announced to Congress by the President. This Doctrine, in its essentials, asserted that the United States of America was opposed (1) "to any non-American action encroaching upon the political independence of American states under any guise, and (2) to the acquisition in any manner of the control of additional territory in the western hemisphere by any non-American power."

General Harrison, from his farm, kept in touch with all these vital events by a steady correspondence with the country's leaders in Washington. His advice was often asked, and he systematically gave it. But now he thought of himself only as a farmer, and never as a general or a politician.

When the new Whig Party was formed in 1834 by influential bankers and industrialists opposed to President Jackson and his sweeping changes, General Harrison became a member. The Whig leaders, looking around for a likely candidate for the Presidential campaign of 1836, chose General Harrison. He accepted reluctantly, ran an indifferent campaign against Martin Van Buren, and was badly defeated.

Four years passed and again it was time for a national election. The Whig party, determined to get rid of Van Buren, met at Harrisburg, Pennsylvania, to choose a candidate for President. Henry Clay, the great statesman and orator, was the party's leader and he fully expected to be the candidate. But the Whig leaders at Harrisburg, after much discussion, decided that Mr. Clay was too controversial as a public figure, and that the party would do better to run a candidate from the West whose public pronouncements on political matters were not so well known, and whose stated views would not infuriate anybody. So they chose General Harrison again, and warned him to conduct his campaign discreetly. Said Nicholas Biddle, one of the Whig leaders, "Let no Committee, no convention, no town meeting, ever extract from him a single word about what he thinks now or what he will do hereafter."

Although General Harrison did not follow to the letter these somewhat cynical instructions, he was prepared to conduct a cautious, if strenuous, campaign for his own election. He did not favor President Van Buren's administration and firmly believed the country needed a new President. He was pleased when the Whig Party nominated, as his running-mate for Vice President, John Tyler, another Virginian with a record of distinguished public service.

The reactions to Harrison's nomination were immediate and loud. When Henry Clay, waiting in his private chambers in Washington, heard the news, he is said to have jumped up, stamped back and forth across the room, and exclaimed wildly: "My friends are not worth the powder and shot it would take to kill them! . . . I am the most unfortunate man in the history of parties: always run by my friends when sure to be defeated, and now betrayed for a nomination when I, or anyone, would be sure of an election."

Martin Van Buren's party of Jacksonian Democrats

were jubilant when they heard that the old frontiersman would oppose their candidate again. They had beaten him once and they expected to beat him again. President Van Buren's supporters became sarcastic and incautious in their newspaper interviews.

"What a joke!" one of them exclaimed to reporters. "Harrison for President! Why, he's just a backwoodsman. He eats corn pone and drinks cider. His mother still lives in a log cabin."

This remark turned out to be the most unfortunate public statement any friend of the elegant Mr. Van Buren ever made.

19 · "Log Cabins and Cider"

General Harrison laughed when he heard about the comment from his rival's political camp.

"It's true," he said, with some amusement, "I eat corn pone whenever I can, because I like it. I also drink cider for the same reason. I am, I suppose, what Mr. Van Buren's party says I am, a backwoodsman. But my mother does not live in a log cabin, though I fail to see what difference it would make if she did. Some of the best people in this country now live, or have lived, in log cabins. It's not *where* a man lives, but *how* he lives that counts."

The principal newspapers of the country printed Van Buren's party's remark and Harrison's reply. The story spread from the *Boston Post* to the *Washington Globe,* from the *Albany Evening Journal* to the *Georgia Argus,* then west to the *Cincinnati Advertiser and Journal* and the *Nashville Union.* Thurlow Weed, a leading Whig politician, cleverly saw how to use the appear in the papers showing Van Buren dining in story to help elect General Harrison. Cartoons began to style on steak and champagne while General Harrison took the simple fare of common people, corn pone and cider.

Before long, all this talk made cider a national beverage. The apple presses throughout the country were never so busy. And log cabins suddenly assumed a new dignity as dwelling places. Speeches and editorials "in praise of log cabins" began to be written and spoken in every state.

One orator, whose flowery speech has come down to us, practically made it seem a disgrace to have been born anywhere else than in a log cabin. Sitting on the same platform with General Harrison at an early political rally, this orator rose and said to the waiting audience, "Log cabins, sirs, were the dwelling places of the founders of our Republic! It was a log cabin that sheltered the daring pioneers of liberty, who exchanged the dangers of the half-sinking *Mayflower* for the perils of a residence in an inhospitable clime."

Warming to his subject, and glancing over at Harrison, whose calm countenance betrayed neither pleasure nor boredom, the orator continued, "It was in view of the Rock of Plymouth, my friends, that the Puritans of New England first erected the log cabins which sheltered the mothers and fathers of a race which now overspreads a continent. It was in a log cabin that the settlers of St. Mary's and of James River first found refuge and protection. It was in log cabins that the pioneers of the mighty West—the Boones, the Worthingtons, the McArthurs, the Shelbys of the Mississippi—reared the race of statesmen and heroes who have since civilized it."

The orator wiped his brow with a large red bandanna, dramatically paused while he tilted a small wooden keg on the rostrum and poured himself a glass of cider, and plunged on with his speech. "Log cabins! Yes, my good friends, it was in a log cabin that the illustrious man before you, General Harrison, [cheers, whoops, and loud applause] the Governor of a territory equal almost in extent to the dominions of the Russian autocrat, learned the lessons of wisdom and courage which have placed him in the foremost rank of the great men of the nation, and are destined to invest him with the highest honors of the Republic [more cheers, whoops, applause]."

"Log cabins, sirs, were the early homes of all the first settlers of every state in the Union. Log cabins were the garrisons of the frontiers, when every acre was won from the wilderness and the savage by the sacrifice of human life! . . . Honored, then, through all time, be these memorials of the trials, the sufferings, the triumphs of our forefathers. Thrice honored be he whom the splendor of palaces . . . the blaze of military and civic renown, could never allure from his attachment to the republican simplicity which he learned beneath the UNHEWN RAFTERS OF HIS LOG CABIN!"

As the orator sat down the audience clapped, stamped, and roared its approval of Harrison and log cabins. Harrison acknowledged the enthusiasm with a wave and a steady smile. When he addressed the audience himself, he tried once to explain that, although he agreed with many of the speaker's remarks in praise of log cabins, they were somewhat exaggerated. True, he said, when he founded his farm at North Bend he had lived a few months in a log cabin, but this cabin had soon been covered with clapboard and was now only a wing of his substantial residence.

The crowd either did not listen, or else mistook his explanation for modesty. They went right ahead roaring out their approval of their backwoods candidate and his plain and simple origin. Even when his rivals pointed out his aristocratic heritage in Virginia and his well-to-do father-in-law, the whole nation went on thinking of him as the "log cabin and cider" candidate.

20 · *"Tippecanoe and Tyler, Too!"*

The campaign for Harrison began to spread like wildfire, and songs by the dozen began to appear about him. These songs all featured Harrison as the "hero of Tippecanoe." Soon the newspapers referred to him as "Old Tip." Someone then coined the slogan "Tippecanoe and Tyler, Too!"

This slogan at once became the rallying cry for the

entire campaign. In effect it said to the voters, "Look, vote the Whig ticket and you can have for President the hero of Tippecanoe, and thrown in for good measure as Vice President, the able statesman, John Tyler, too!"

As "Tippecanoe and Tyler, Too" banners began to appear everywhere, with accompanying songs, the campaign of 1840 took on a wilder enthusiasm. General Harrison tramped the country making speeches and, with each speech, made hundreds of new friends. In Ohio companies of soldiers began to turn out in uniform to see the General. The Putnam Grays, the Warren Greens, the Buckeye Rangers—these formed into line and marched behind a blaring brass band in a great parade in honor of General Harrison. Leading each parade was a wagon drawn by twenty-four oxen, with a miniature log cabin on the wagon frame and a barrel of cider in front. Often live 'coons played on the roof of the cabin as it went along.

With all this parading and banner-waving and cider-drinking, the voters began to have fun. Soon every community that did not boast a log cabin started to put one up. Volunteers brought their axes into the forests and cut and shaped the logs. A double team of oxen then dragged in a fifty-foot ridgepole. The men, working from sunup to sunset, usually could build a cabin in one day.

To make the whole event a real social spree, the local town guilds, committees, and ladies' societies pitched in to help. The women, who called themselves "Tippecanoers," prepared the food for the men working on the log cabin.

If there was a man who was too lazy or too weak to swing an ax, he was required, before he was fed, to sing a Tippecanoe song or to play an instrument for the general entertainment. Red-uniformed men from volunteer fire departments supervised the huge bonfires of shavings and logs that were set burning at sundown. Pine torches and large saucers containing wicks fed by whale oil provided the light for supper, dancing, and the speech-making that followed.

The local fiddlers played the entire day. To the tune of "Rosin the Bow" and "Highland Laddie" and "The Little Pig's Tail" the crowd sang songs about "Old Tip." One song ended with the words, "With Tip and Tyler we'll bust Van's biler!"

Van Buren's party soon became alarmed by the

The campaign for Harrison spread like wildfire.

clamor and cheerful hullaballoo gathering around Harrison's name. The *Baltimore Republican,* in bold letters on its front page, advised the voters to give Harrison a barrel of cider "and a pension of $2,000 a year and let him withdraw as a candidate. Do this and we wager he will sit the remainder of his days in a log cabin by the side of a fire and study moral philosophy. Pray let him do so. The country would thus be better served than to have this farmer in the White House!"

But the voters of the West had no intention of letting their hero "sit by the fire." They were proud to think of Harrison as a farmer. Placards like the following began to appear. *"George Washington Was a Farmer, William Henry Harrison Is a Farmer.* Like causes produce like effects. The country was prosperous under Washington. Let us have another farmer President and another age of Prosperity and Plenty."

At Lafayette, Indiana, on the site of the battle of Tippecanoe, 30,000 people assembled on May 29, 1840, to hail General Harrison. They came by boat, horse, carriage, and on foot from three states. They camped in tents, or slept in their wagons. They had come for one purpose: to see "Old Tip," to shake his hand, and to assure him of their votes.

A famous cartoon of this event, the largest political rally that had ever been held in the United States, shows General Harrison cordially welcoming two of his old soldier comrades in front of a log cabin. Even Harrison's dog, which is prominent in the picture, repeats the welcome by a hearty and significant wag of his tail.

But all of the writings, speeches, songs, log-cabin raisings and parades, though more active and merrier than anything that had happened before in political campaigns, were not as effective and dramatic as the "ball-rolling" stunt which got under way for Harrison late in the election year.

It all happened spontaneously, and by a great stroke of luck. Some orator in Baltimore made the remark that the enthusiasm for Harrison was sweeping the country. The orator who followed him said, "Well, let's keep the ball rolling!" A listener went home and appeared at the next rally with a huge rubber ball ten feet in diameter and covered with stout leather. On the ball were the words, "This ball we roll, with all our soul, for Tippecanoe and Tyler, too!" Everyone laughed and joined the man to roll the ball through the streets of the city. Someone then got the idea of "keeping the ball rolling" by pushing it to the next town.

Shortly thereafter great rubber balls were being pushed throughout the twenty-six states. From village to village, from Penobscot to Mississippi, from Portland to Savannah, from New York to Fort Dearborn, great crowds could be seen "rolling the ball" merrily down the roads, usually with a flag and a band accompanying them. Sometimes the "ball-rollers" dressed as Indians and war-whooped as they rolled, to the delight of everybody. At once a song sprang up to celebrate the new fad. It was not a very good song, but people sang it anyway.

Oh, what has caused the great commotion
Motion, motion, the country through?
It is the ball
A-rolling on,
For Tippecanoe and Tyler, Too.

The ladies, too, God bless their souls,
Souls, souls, souls, the country through,
Will to a man,
Do all they can,
For Tippecanoe and Tyler, Too.

Martin Van Buren saw what was happening. In an attempt to compete with "Old Tippecanoe" he adopted the signature "Old Kinderhook," the name of his Dutch-style home. He signed many cartoons and political pamphlets with the letters O.K. For some reason these two letters caught the popular imagination. Though they did not help Van Buren greatly in his fight for office, they have remained in the language as a colloquial term meaning "all right." So, with this rousing political campaign, "keep the ball rolling" and "okay" got into the American language to stay.

21 · "Old Tip" Becomes President

The great campaign of 1840, with all its colorful songs, parades, and speeches, ended happily for William Henry Harrison. He was elected ninth President of the United States by a tremendous popular vote. The whole country celebrated, especially the newer Ohio River states where the pioneers were proud to have a President who understood and represented them.

In February of 1841, Harrison started to Washington,

via Philadelphia and Baltimore, to get ready for his inaugural address and to be sworn in as the new President. His trip East was a triumphal journey. Bells rang in every city to signalize his arrival. Crowds turned out to wave and cheer.

The city of Washington prepared a constant round of brilliant receptions, dinners, and soirées in his honor. One dinner was held in a great log-cabin hall where 1,800 wax candles and tapers burned a flaming welcome to the old hero.

President Harrison smiled and bowed his way through all these festivities. He was 67 years old now, but his back was straight and his eyes were clear. Only Anna, his wife, saw that underneath his firm military exterior his body was beginning to weaken. She persuaded him to leave Washington for a five-day rest in Virginia before inaugural day.

March 4, 1841, dawned cold and dreary in the Capitol City. Nevertheless, Pennsylvania Avenue in Washington was lined with people to cheer "Old Tip" on the official day he was to become President. Not since George Washington's inauguration had the public demonstrated so much enthusiasm.

Hundreds of soldiers and sailors, led by blaring bands

and high-stepping flag corps, led the procession to the speaker's stand. Tippecanoe clubs and societies displayed their banners. Young students and schoolboys rode past on decorated log-cabin wagons, with streamers trailing the ground behind. Mottoes waved from the buildings asserting that "Old Tip's Cabin is Up!" Most of the women and girls packing the avenue wore "Tippecanoe scarves," with log cabins, axes, "keys to the West," and Indian heads stitched, or painted, on them.

When President Harrison rose to speak it took ten full minutes to quiet the cheering audience. He addressed the crowd for over an hour. He loved to speak and the people loved to hear him. Only the professional politicians became restless. Daniel Webster, who had voted for Harrison, remarked that "Old Tip took a long time to say very little." But then Webster was a famous orator himself. He often said that he preferred the sound of his own voice to all others. He was not a good listener.

Actually, President Harrison said a number of things that his supporters were pleased to hear. He pledged pensions for old soldiers and they whooped with joy. He pledged grants of free lands for pioneers to the West. The pioneers cheered. He pledged to hold office for one term only. The crowd groaned. He pledged not to give out jobs right and left to government office-seekers as President Jackson had done under his "spoils system." This remark got broken applause, for there were many office-seekers in the crowd.

On the not yet burning question of slavery in the several states, President Harrison took the position that slavery was not a government affair. He thought it rather a matter for the individual states to decide. The Southerners in the crowd cheered him. A few abolitionists booed.

At the end of his speech he gave his personal philosophy about the duties of citizenship. He took as his theme his belief that in the ideal government "every citizen was a soldier."

"The whole secret of ancient military glory," he said in a ringing voice, "the foundation of that wonderful military skill and exalted valor which enabled the petty Republic of Athens to resist the mighty torrent of Persian invasion, which formed the walls of Sparta, and conducted the Roman legions to the conquest of the world, will be found in the military education of our youth!"

Then, with a final plea for "a larger measure of accord and harmony in public affairs," the old General sat down.

The crowd stood in the rain clapping their hands and howling their pleasure. The oath of office was then administered, a prayer was said, the bands started up again, and the ceremony was over. A new President was in the White House.

President Harrison began his demanding job as the country's leader in a flurry of activity. His office door was open to everyone who had a sensible reason to see him. Consequently, a stream of people came and went every day through the White House door. Soon all this coming and going began to wear down his vitality. His wife warned him again, but the President seemed unable to guard his strength. He felt he could never deny an audience to a worthy visitor. As the President of a democratic country, he believed it was his duty always to be available.

A British traveler in Washington at this time has left the best pen-portrait of the President's character and attitude toward his many callers. Said the observant Britisher, "President Harrison's natural kindness was seen at every moment. Whoever called to pay him a visit was sure to be asked to dinner; whoever called for a place or position was sure to get a promise; whoever hinted at a want of money was sure to get a draft. It soon became common talk that the President was overdrawing his account, over-promising his partisans, and overfeeding his friends. Also, he was overtaxing his strength."

How true this last observation was! On March 28, 1841, the President, as usual, went out to market early —he always shopped for the household food—but when he came home this day he walked slowly. By the time he got to the White House he had contracted a chill. The chill turned into pneumonia in his weakened body. Seven days later, on April 4th, only one month after he had been elected, President Harrison died.

His last recorded words, which the newspapers gave to a mourning nation, show that even at the end his thoughts were of his country. "Sir," the old Soldier-President said to Vice-President John Tyler, who was at his bedside, "I wish you to understand the principles of government. I wish them carried out. I ask nothing more."

President Harrison was buried in the old Congressional cemetery in Washington. But in June of the same year his devoted family had his remains removed to North Bend, Ohio.

His tomb stands there today. It looks out over the country he loved, out over the quietly flowing Ohio River and the rolling hills of the vast territory the gallant "Old Tip" saved for America.

Index

LANDMARK BOOKS

1 **The Voyages of Christopher Columbus** by Armstrong Sperry
2 **The Landing of the Pilgrims** by James Daugherty
3 **Pocahontas and Captain John Smith** by Marie Lawson
4 **Paul Revere and the Minute Men** by Dorothy Canfield Fisher
5 **Our Independence and the Constitution** by Dorothy Canfield Fisher
6 **The California Gold Rush** by May McNeer
7 **The Pony Express** by Samuel Hopkins Adams
8 **Lee and Grant at Appomattox** by MacKinlay Kantor
9 **The Building of the First Transcontinental Railroad** by Adele Nathan
10 **The Wright Brothers** by Quentin Reynolds
11 **Prehistoric America** by Anne Terry White
12 **The Vikings** by Elizabeth Janeway
13 **The Santa Fe Trail** by Samuel Hopkins Adams
14 **The Story of the U. S. Marines** by George Hunt
15 **The Lewis and Clark Expedition** by Richard L. Neuberger
16 **The Monitor and the Merrimac** by Fletcher Pratt
17 **The Explorations of Père Marquette** by Jim Kjelgaard
18 **The Panama Canal** by Bob Considine
19 **The Pirate Lafitte and the Battle of New Orleans** by Robert Tallant
20 **Custer's Last Stand** by Quentin Reynolds
21 **Daniel Boone** by John Mason Brown
22 **Clipper Ship Days** by John Jennings
23 **Gettysburg** by MacKinlay Kantor
24 **The Louisiana Purchase** by Robert Tallant
25 **Wild Bill Hickok Tames the West** by Stewart H. Holbrook
26 **Betsy Ross and the Flag** by Jane Mayer
27 **The Conquest of the North and South Poles** by Russell Owen
28 **Ben Franklin of Old Philadelphia** by Margaret Cousins
29 **Trappers and Traders of the Far West** by James Daugherty
30 **Mr. Bell Invents the Telephone** by Katherine Shippen
31 **The Barbary Pirates** by C. S. Forester
32 **Sam Houston, The Tallest Texan** by William Johnson
33 **The Winter at Valley Forge** by Van Wyck Mason
34 **The Erie Canal** by Samuel Hopkins Adams
35 **Thirty Seconds Over Tokyo** by Ted Lawson and Bob Considine
36 **Thomas Jefferson** by Vincent Sheean
37 **The Coming of the Mormons** by Jim Kjelgaard
38 **George Washington Carver** by Anne Terry White
39 **John Paul Jones** by Armstrong Sperry
40 **The First Overland Mail** by Robert Pinkerton
41 **Teddy Roosevelt and the Rough Riders** by Henry Castor
42 **To California by Covered Wagon** by George R. Stewart
43 **Peter Stuyvesant of Old New York** by Anna and Russel Crouse
44 **Lincoln and Douglas** by Regina Z. Kelly
45 **Robert Fulton and the Steamboat** by Ralph Nading Hill
46 **The F.B.I.** by Quentin Reynolds
47 **Dolly Madison** by Jane Mayer
48 **John James Audubon** by Margaret and John Kieran
49 **Hawaii** by Oscar Lewis
50 **War Chief of the Seminoles** by May McNeer
51 **Old Ironsides, The Fighting *Constitution*** by Harry Hansen
52 **The Mississippi Bubble** by Thomas B. Costain
53 **Kit Carson and the Wild Frontier** by Ralph Moody
54 **Robert E. Lee and the Road of Honor** by Hodding Carter
55 **Guadalcanal Diary** by Richard Tregaskis
56 **Commodore Perry and the Opening of Japan** by Ferdinand Kuhn
57 **Davy Crockett** by Stewart H. Holbrook
58 **Clara Barton, Founder of the American Red Cross** by Helen Dore Boylston
59 **The Story of San Francisco** by Charlotte Jackson
60 **Up the Trail from Texas** by J. Frank Dobie
61 **Abe Lincoln: Log Cabin to White House** by Sterling North
62 **The Story of D-Day: June 6, 1944** by Bruce Bliven, Jr.
63 **Rogers' Rangers and the French and Indian War** by Bradford Smith
64 **The World's Greatest Showman: The Life of P. T. Barnum** by J. Bryan III
65 **Sequoyah: Leader of the Cherokees** by Alice Marriott
66 **Ethan Allen and the Green Mountain Boys** by Slater Brown
67 **Wyatt Earp: U. S. Marshal** by Stewart H. Holbrook
68 **The Early Days of Automobiles** by Elizabeth Janeway
69 **The Witchcraft of Salem Village** by Shirley Jackson
70 **The West Point Story** by Colonel Red Reeder & Nardi Reeder Campion

LANDMARK BOOKS *continued*

71 George Washington: Frontier Colonel by Sterling North

72 The Texas Rangers by Will Henry

73 Buffalo Bill's Great Wild West Show by Walter Havighurst

74 Evangeline and the Acadians by Robert Tallant

75 The Story of the Secret Service by Ferdinand Kuhn

76 Tippecanoe and Tyler, Too! by Stanley Young

77 America's First World War by Henry Castor

78 The Doctors Who Conquered Yellow Fever by Ralph Nading Hill

WORLD LANDMARK BOOKS

W-1 The First Men in the World by Anne Terry White

W-2 Alexander the Great by John Gunther

W-3 Adventures and Discoveries of Marco Polo by Richard J. Walsh

W-4 Joan of Arc by Nancy Wilson Ross

W-5 King Arthur and His Knights by Mabel L. Robinson

W-6 Mary, Queen of Scots by Emily Hahn

W-7 Napoleon and the Battle of Waterloo by Frances Winwar

W-8 Royal Canadian Mounted Police by Richard L. Neuberger

W-9 The Man Who Changed China by Pearl S. Buck

W-10 The Battle of Britain by Quentin Reynolds

W-11 The Crusades by Anthony West

W-12 Genghis Khan and the Mongol Horde by Harold Lamb

W-13 Queen Elizabeth and the Spanish Armada by Frances Winwar

W-14 Simón Bolívar by Arnold Whitridge

W-15 The Slave Who Freed Haiti by Katharine Scherman

W-16 The Story of Scotland Yard by Laurence Thompson

W-17 The Life of Saint Patrick by Quentin Reynolds

W-18 The Exploits of Xenophon by Geoffrey Household

W-19 Captain Cook Explores the South Seas by Armstrong Sperry

W-20 Marie Antoinette by Bernardine Kielty

W-21 Will Shakespeare and the Globe Theater by Anne Terry White

W-22 The French Foreign Legion by Wyatt Blassingame

W-23 Martin Luther by Harry Emerson Fosdick

W-24 The Hudson's Bay Company by Richard Morenus

W-25 Balboa: Swordsman and Conquistador by Felix Riesenberg, Jr.

W-26 The Magna Charta by James Daugherty

W-27 Leonardo da Vinci by Emily Hahn

W-28 General Brock and Niagara Falls by Samuel Hopkins Adams

W-29 Catherine the Great by Katharine Scherman

W-30 The Fall of Constantinople by Bernardine Kielty

W-31 Ferdinand Magellan by Seymour Gates Pond

W-32 Garibaldi: Father of Modern Italy by Marcia Davenport

W-33 The Story of Albert Schweitzer by Anita Daniel

Date Due

May 28	AG 5 '92		
NOV 14 1964	JAN 22 '97		
DEC 21 1964	JUN 30 98		
FEB 8 1967	JY 13 '00		
May 11 1967	NO 02 '00		
DEC 10 1968	AG 08 '05		
DEC 24 1968			
FEB 12 1969			
FEB 27 1969			
MAR 29 '72			
JAN 16 1973			
JUN 23 1975			
FEB 01 1984			

Young, Stanley
Tippecanoe and Tyler, too!